Fabulous
FUN WITH PUZZLES

Fun and mental gymnastics of every kind for everybody
Brain Twisters • Word and Anagram Puzzles • Pencil and Paper
Challenges • Cut-out and Put-together Testers • Mathematical and
Number Posers • Problems with Coins, Counters, and Matches

Fabulous FUN with PUZZLES

by Joseph Leeming

Time Inc.
HOME ENTERTAINMENT

Edited, designed, & illustrated by Patrick Merrell

Time Inc. Home Entertainment

Publisher: Richard Fraiman
General Manager: Steven Sandonato
Executive Director, Marketing Services: Carol Pittard
Director, Retail & Special Sales: Tom Mifsud
Director, New Product Development: Peter Harper
Assistant Director, Brand Marketing: Laura Adam
Associate Counsel: Helen Wan
Marketing Manager: Victoria Alfonso
Senior Brand Manager, TWRS/M: Holly Oakes
Design & Prepress Manager: Anne-Michelle Gallero
Book Production Manager: Susan Chodakiewicz

Published by Time Inc. Home Entertainment

Time Inc.
1271 Avenue of the Americas
New York, New York 10020

Special Thanks:

Alexandra Bliss
Glenn Buonocore
Jon Delfin
Margaret Hess
Suzanne Janso
Dennis Marcel
Robert Marasco
Brooke Reger
Mary Sarro-Waite
Ilene Schreider
Adriana Tierno
Alex Voznesenskiy

We welcome your comments and suggestions about *Fabulous Fun with Puzzles*. Please write us at:

Fabulous Fun with Puzzles
Attention: Book Editors
PO Box 11016
Des Moines, IA 50336-1016

ISBN 10: 1-60320-034-7
ISBN 13: 978-1-60320-034-9

Library of Congress Control Number: 2008902953

Time Inc. Home Entertainment is a subsidiary of Time Inc.

The activities in this book are intended for adults or to be performed under adult supervision.
Under no circumstances should a child be permitted to handle matchsticks without appropriate adult supervision.
All activities in this book are performed at your own risk.

Table of CONTENTS

Introduction

There are very few forms of mental amusement that can be as absorbingly interesting or stimulating as good puzzles. Their successful solution requires close concentration, imagination, logical reasoning, and clear, correlated thinking. Each puzzle is a new test, a new game that can be fun for one, or passed on to friends to become a source of interest or amusement for many.

For many people, puzzles provide an outlet for pent-up wit and intelligence that do not have a means of expression during the daily round. They open up a new and different world, in which we can roam at will, pitting our wits against the thinkers — old and new — whose minds conceived these ofttimes tortuous devices of bafflement. Because of their very nature and reason for being, each puzzle is a challenge, and our satisfaction in solving it is as intense and rewarding as winning a closely contested game.

— *Joseph Leeming*

In 1946, Joseph Leeming created *Fun With Puzzles* and the next year, *More Fun With Puzzles*. Now, more than half a century later, his two timeless collections of conundrums and posers have been combined into the book you're holding, updated and refined.

The challenges are varied, in both content and difficulty. You'll find forgotten classics and original creations, humorous teasers and logical testers, easy ticklers and confounding head scratchers. And just when you think you've caught on to all the devious angles from which Mr. Leeming's puzzles come at you, a new twist will arise. Prepare to be continually bemused, amused, and amazed.

Born in 1897, Joseph Leeming served in both Burma and Afghanistan as an information officer for the U.S. State Department. He was also a writer of children's books and books on maritime matters and religion. In addition to his popular *Fun With* series, he wrote *Brave Ships of World War II*, *The White House in Picture and Story*, *Ships and Cargoes*, and *Yoga and the Bible*. His winters were spent in Punjab, India, and in 1968 he died at the age of 71 in Folkestone, England.

It is one of man's curious idiosyncracies to create difficulties for the pleasure of resolving them.

— Joseph de Maistre
French political philosopher (1753-1821)

Word and Letter PUZZLES

1

DOUBLE TIME

There are many words that contain double letters, such as the word "letter" itself. Words with double t, double s, and double e are plentiful, but when it comes to double i or double w, examples are few and far between. See if you can think of words containing these double letters (no proper names):

1. double a (but not at the beginning of the word)
2. double h
3. double i
4. double k
5. double u
6. double v
7. double w

2

WHAT'S THE WORD?

There is a six-letter word that has the letter l in the middle, in the beginning, and at the end. But there is only one l in the word. Can you figure out what the word is?

Read this one very carefully before you give up. There's a catch.

3

NO SEE NO SAW

This is a hard one, but a good one to try on your friends. See if they, or you for that matter, can make a seven-word sentence out of this:

NO ONE SAW IT NO SAW

4

BURIED PROVERB

The words from a familiar proverb have been buried in the following sentences. The first word (which is the only one that is just one letter long) is buried in the first sentence, the second word is buried in the second sentence, and so on. Can you uncover the six-word proverb?

1. A bad cat ran away.
2. He found a scroll in gathering up the papers.
3. It is the best one that I have ever seen.
4. The rug at her summer house is a valuable one.
5. He is an old friend of mine.
6. Amos soon saw through the odd stratagem.

5

THE ABSURD WORD

There is a 13-letter word that means "a condition where one has no bodily feeling." It can also be a synonym of "absurdity." It contains only one vowel, but this occurs four times, one consonant that occurs six times, another consonant that occurs twice, and a third consonant that occurs just once. Can you figure out what the word is?

6

Q QUIZ

See if you can think of a five-letter word beginning with Q that would fit each of the following clues. Can you think of two for the last one?

1. serenity	7. type of pen	13. allotment	19. carton amount
2. line	8. question	14. cite	20. campus areas
3. a bird	9. odd	15. hearty draft	21. misgiving
4. sort of	10. entirely	16. search	22. Caine captain
5. tremble	11. hive head	17. speedy	23. witticisms
6. phony doc	12. oddity	18. blanket	24. suppress

7

THE TEN WORDS

Many well-known people, including writers, editors, and others who constantly deal with words, have tried their hands at spelling the ten words below, but very few of them have succeeded in getting more than seven of them right. In fact, we've spelled one of the words incorrectly. First, see if you can you find that word. Then read the list aloud to your friends and see how many they can spell correctly. Odds are they won't get all ten.

inoculate	embarrass	harass	supersede	innuendo
rarefy	vilify	mispelled	desiccate	picnicking

8

I SEE A LOT OF THAT

Punctuate the following sentence, so as to create six sentences that make sense:

That that is is that that is not is not that that is is not that that is not that that is not is not that that is is that not so it is

9

HAD ENOUGH?

See if you can punctuate the following sentence so that it makes sense:

John where James had had had had had had had had had had had a better effect on the teacher

10

ER...WHAT DOES IT SAY?

What phrase is represented by the following:

er and **er**

11

BEHEADINGS

To behead a word means to take away its first letter. See how you do with these beheadings:

    1. Behead a common ink color and leave a shortcoming.
    2. Behead a shelf and leave a rim.
    3. Behead a church doctrine and leave a marsh stalk.
    4. Behead an atmospheric layer and leave a belt.
    5. Behead a pronoun and leave a royal successor.
    6. Behead a hard blow and leave something a camel has.

12

CAN YOU READ IT?

See if you can make one sentence out of the following, taking into account the positions of the various words:

stand	take	to	taking
I	you	throw	my

13

GHOTI

This is a somewhat different kind of a word puzzle. The problem is to find a common English word that is represented by these letters: GHOTI. To get the answer, you must find different pronunciations for letters or groups of letters contained in the word GHOTI. As a starter, the first letter in the answer is "f," which represents "gh" as it is pronounced in "enough."

14

THE FOUR ADJECTIVES

There are only four commonly used adjectives in the English language that end in "dous." See if you can name them.

15

ARE YOU SAGE?

Can you quickly come up with three words that each contain "sage" in consecutive order? We've assembled a list of 15 such words in the answer section, 10 of which are common.

16

LITTLE WORDS FROM BIG ONES

This type of puzzle is sometimes called "the word game" and is undoubtedly one of the most intriguing ways to while away time on a rainy day, a lazy summer afternoon, one of those long winter evenings, or on a railroad journey. The puzzle is to see how many smaller words you can make out of one big one. A list of answers is not given in the back. Instead, the number of small words that you should try to find is given here with each word. Words should be three letters or longer.

CONSOLIDATE	at least 59 words
ADHESIVE	at least 30 words
BELLIGERENT	at least 21 words
INTOLERABLE	at least 37 words
EMPHATIC	at least 48 words
PROBABLE	at least 33 words
WASTREL	at least 26 words
HIEROGLYPHICS	at least 20 words
INVETERATE	at least 31 words
INTELLIGENT	at least 27 words
CAPTIVATE	at least 36 words
INGREDIENT	at least 17 words
REPOSITORY	at least 27 words
SCINTILLATE	at least 35 words
TABULATE	at least 22 words
PALPITATE	at least 18 words
SENTIMENTAL	at least 39 words
MISCELLANEOUS	at least 53 words

17

HOW'S YOUR SPANISH?

See if you can name the United States cities and states represented by these translations of their real names, which are Spanish:

1. the angels   2. tall pole   3. holy faith   4. flowery   5. snow-covered

18

THE WORD PYRAMID

In this puzzle seven letters — M S R E T S A — will form seven different words. Start by putting a one-letter word in the top square. Beneath it put a two-letter word, using the letter in the top square plus one other letter from the list. Beneath this put a three-letter word, using the two-letter word plus one additional, unused letter. Continue on in this manner until you've filled the bottom squares with a word that uses all seven letters. Letters from a preceding word do not need to be used in the same order in your new word. Can you find more than one way?

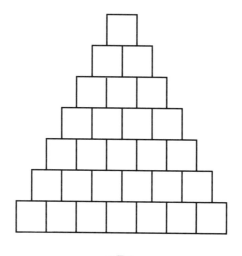

19

FOUR-LETTER PUZZLE

See if you can think of a four-letter word that ends in "eny."

20

THE MISSING LETTER PUZZLE

In the following poem one letter, a vowel, has been left out. See if you can discover which vowel it is and then insert it in the many places where it belongs so that the poem will make sense.

W h t m r s l n d s o s d l y s w r ?
    W h t d y s s d r k s d y s t h t w r l r m ?
l s ! s k n y , s k t h n d , f r ,
    l l s h l l c l l w r h r s s n d h r m .
W h y c l l , s b l l d s t l k , t h t g h s t l y r t
    l l g l l n t c t s — g r n d n d m n l y p r t .

21

ALPHABET SENTENCES

The puzzle is to make a sentence as short as possible that contains all the letters of the alphabet. See if you can make any that are shorter than the ones given in the answer section of this book.

22

BURIED POETS

The names of eight British poets are buried in the following poem, one in each line. See if you can find them.

The sun is darting rays of gold
    Upon the moor, enchanting spot
Whose purple heights by Ronald loved,
    Up open to his shepherd cot.

And sundry denizens of the air
    Are flying, aye each to his nest;
A skyward hike at such an hour,
    Once there to mend on needed rest.

23

CONCEALED LETTERS

How many and what letters of the alphabet are concealed in this diagram? Only letters that are normally drawn with straight lines qualify.

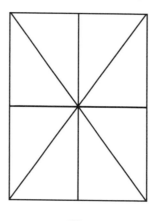

24

WORD ENIGMAS

See if you can decipher the following. Warning — they're tricky.

$$\frac{R\,I\,O}{T A} = \text{a seven-letter geographical name}$$
$$\frac{T}{S} = \text{a ten-letter word}$$

25

ABC-TUMBLE DOWN D

This is an old favorite in some parts of the country and yet unknown in others. The puzzle is to read these letters in such a way so as to make a conversation between two people.

"A B C D Q T T?"
"O M N O Q T T."
"O S A R A B C M?"
"O G I C M."
"S A R L N L C N L O E E."

26

ANIMAL KINGDOM

Listed below are 19 clues, each followed by two capital letters. The puzzle is to fill in two words that start with the capital letters given. The first word must match the clue; the second must be an animal, bird or insect that sounds like the first word but is spelled differently. #1 has been done as an example.

If you want to make a game out of this, count 5 points for each correct answer, and the high scorer will be the winner. A score of 55 is fair, 70 to 80 is good, and 85 or more is exceptional.

1. to exist   B e_____ and B ee_____
2. naked   B_____ and B_____
3. paste for bread   D_____ and D_____
4. expensive   D_____ and D_____
5. run for it   F_____ and F_____
6. throaty   H_____ and H_____
7. was aware of   K_____ and G_____
8. long, thin candle   T_____ and T_____
9. line   R_____ and R_____
10. not me   Y_____ and E_____
11. they make a chain   L_____ and L_____
12. eyebrows, e.g.   H_____ and H_____
13. spoke like a Scot   B_____ and B_____
14. gain by work   E_____ and E_____
15. animal's hole   B_____ and B_____
16. whimper   M_____ and M_____
17. goat-man of myth   F_____ and F_____
18. rougher   C_____ and C_____
19. atmospheric state   W_____ and W_____

27

WHAT'S THIS?

What phrase of three words can you make of the word "ALLO"?

28

SPELLING BEE

Start with any letter in the square below. Move one square at a time in any direction (including diagonally) until you have spelled out a common English word of four or more letters. You can't revisit the same letter to spell a word. Also, do not use proper names or form plurals by adding "S" to a three-letter word. Par on this one is 20 words in 30 minutes. Our answer list includes 28 words, including one 10-letter word.

C	A	Q	H	S
B	N	R	U	K
S	G	V	L	O
W	T	M	I	P
Z	Y	E	D	J

29

THE YY SENTENCE

What poem of 16 words do the following letters make?

YY U R, YY U B;
I C U R YY 4 me.

30

THE PROFESSOR'S PUZZLE

A professor who specialized in Latin was puzzled one day to discover the following inscription on a narrow, upright stone by a Vermont roadside. At first he was confused, but then the light dawned. Can you figure it out?

TOTI
EMUL
ESTO

31

ONE-LETTER WORDS

Each of these clues can be answered with a single letter. Can you "C" the way to get all 14 answers? A different letter must be used for each answer.

1. a vegetable
2. a drink
3. a body of water
4. a command to a horse
5. a sensory organ
6. be in debt
7. a river in Scotland
8. building addition
9. a bird
10. a woman's name
11. a verb used with "we"
12. an actor's signal
13. an insect
14. a puzzle solver

32

TWO-LETTER WORDS

See if you can come up with an answer to each of these clues using two letters. The two letters, when said aloud, must sound like the correct answer. For example, the answer to #1 is IC or "icy."

1. chilly
2. overage
3. rot
4. not hard
5. vacant
6. composition
7. run-down
8. stand out
9. octogenarian's age
10. results
11. jealousy
12. tent in the Old West

33

MORE-LETTER WORDS

Now see if you can write the answer to each of these clues using three letters or, in the last case, five letters.

1. happiness
2. foe
3. a small boy has lots of it
4. appropriateness for the task (5 letters)

34

THE TYPEWRITER'S TOP ROW

The top row of lettered keys on the standard typewriter has the following letters: QWERTYUIOP. It is possible to make four 10-letter words from the letters in this group. Not all the letters are used, while some of them are used more than once. One of the words, curiously enough, is "typewriter." Can you come up with any one of the others?

35

WORD MAKING

Here's a test of your word-making skills. With each batch of letters below, see if you can match the totals specified. (No proper names.)

1. A E G R T: 13 three-letter words and 5 four-letter words
2. E I L V: 4 four-letter words
3. A E K S T: 5 five-letter words
4. O P S T: 6 four-letter words
5. A P R S T: 15 four-letter words and 4 five-letter words
6. S A I L D O N G R E W: spell a single word

36

WORD GROWING PAINS

Seven clues are listed below. The puzzle is to find an answer to the first clue that is one letter long, an answer to the second clue that is two letters long, and so on. Additionally, each answer must contains all the letters in the preceding answer (in the *same order*) plus one additional letter. The added letter may be inserted anywhere in the word. For example, the answer to #1 is "a" and #2 is "at," adding "t" to the first answer.

1. an article
2. a preposition
3. consumed
4. assess

5. container with slats
6. produce
7. reduce to ashes

Here are another seven words to work on:

1. an article
2. commercial
3. also
4. acreage
5. like highways
6. shaved smooth
7. made arrangements

Follow the same procedure with these eight clues:

1. a pronoun
2. a preposition
3. transgress
4. utter musical sounds
5. move to and fro while suspended
6. fastening with thread
7. slowly cooking
8. throwing irregularly

37

WORD ENIGMAS

Word enigmas are fascinating puzzles that rate as favorites with many people. Use the clues to arrive at your solution. For example, the first clue below tells us that the 4th and 5th letters are "n" and "o."

A. I am a word of 5 letters —
    without my 1, 2, 3, I am a negative
    without my 3, 5, I am a seamstress's item
    without my 1, 5, I am a Scottish man's first name
    without my 2, 5, I am a kitchen utensil
    without my 1, 3, 5, I am a preposition
    my whole is a musical instrument

B. I am a word of 8 letters —
    without my 3, 4, 5, I am a sharp pain
    without my 1, 2, 3, 4, I am a sovereign
    without my 6, 7, 8, I am a supply
    without my 2, 6, 7, 8, I am an article of apparel
    without my 2, 3, 4, 8, I am a surface membrane
    my whole is an article of apparel

C. I am a word of 7 letters —
without my 1, 5, 7, I am a garment
without my 2, 4, 5, 7, I am an American poet
without my 1, 4, 7, I am a part
without my 4, 5, I am a preface
without my 5, 7, I am an inquiry
my whole is a difficult matter

D. I am a word of 6 letters —
without my 5, 6, I am a scheme
without my 1, 6, I am a narrow path
without my 5, I am something that grows
without my 2, 4, 5, I am a small square
without my 1, 2, 5, I am an insect
my whole is a heavenly body

38

LETTER ADDING

In the following letter-adding puzzles, you must use the clues to discover the target word defined on the first line. The letter mentioned in each clue is always added to the front of the target word.

A. Alone, I suffer —
with B, I become a type of payment
with F, I become a simple grade
with M, I become letters
with N, I become a fastener
with P, I become a carrier
with R, I become a handhold
with S, I become a sight at sea
with T, I become a wagger
with W, I become a moan

B. Alone, I am a direction —
with B, I become a wild animal

with F, I become a sumptuous repast
with L, I become minimal
with Y, I become a fungal growth

C. Alone, I am a word of obligation —
with B, I become purchased
with F, I become battled
with S, I become looked for

D. Alone, I am what people do to subsist —
with B, I become a rhythm
with F, I become a difficult performance
with H, I become warmth
with M, I become food
with N, I become tidy
with P, I become a fuel source
with S, I become a place to rest

39

ANIMAL ADDITIONS

Each of the following problems, when correctly guessed, results in a homophone for the name of an animal, bird, or insect.

For example: A. A. Milne bear + a parent =
Answer: Pooh + ma = puma

1. building part + bad grade + an insect =
2. member of a monastic order + lock opener =
3. mammal covering + not out =
4. small piece + religious man =
5. river in Italy + part of the leg =
6. cross home plate + a small vegetable + atop =
7. pig's flesh + an evergreen tree + another evergreen tree =
8. a girl's name + performed =
9. fence of bushes + pig =

40

WORD ADDITIONS

See if you can figure out the words, which when spoken, make these problems true.

1. supporting + melody + black billiard ball = lucky
2. word of greeting + put on a scale = public road
3. surprised sound + part of the leg = large body of water
4. bridge complement + a hot beverage + giant's syllable = make strong
5. wrong + scorch = genuine

41

WORD SUBTRACTIONS

Here's a trickier challenge. What words will make these word subtraction problems true? Unlike the previous two puzzles, the exact spelling of the words, not just the way they sound, is used.

For example: transmitting - conclusion = utter musically
Answer: sending - end = sing

1. apportioned - certain = honeyed drink
2. inexpensive - a pronoun = head covering
3. wedding figure - purge = to exist
4. with complete honesty - rating = an insect
5. attired in - a sense organ = plane part

42

EASY DOES IT

Although this one is fairly simple, it can sometimes take quite a bit of work to solve. All you have to do is to rearrange the following letters so that they will spell the name of a living creature:

BRINO

43

FORWARD AND BACKWARD

Each of the following sentences describes one word when its letters are read forward and another one entirely when the letters are read backward.

1. Read forward I am there in person; read backward I am wicked.
2. Read forward I am set down; read backward I am a part on a radio.
3. Read forward I am kitchen utensils; read backward I am a fastener.
4. Read forward I am 40 winks; read backward I am rinds.
5. Read forward I am components; read backward I am a purse feature.
6. Read forward I am a civil wrong; read backward I am a gait.
7. Read forward I am cozy; read backward I am weapons.
8. Read forward I am an outdoor game; read backward I am to whip.
9. Read forward I am a celestial body; read backward I am rodents.
10. Read forward I am metal canisters; read backward I am a bad mood.

44

WORD TRANSFORMATIONS

The object of a word transformation puzzle is to change a given word to another by altering one letter at a time, each time forming a new word.

For example, changing DOG to CAT in 3 moves could be done this way: dog, dot, cot, cat. Now try these:

1. EAST to WEST in 3 moves
2. BOY to MAN in 3 moves
3. HATE to LOVE in 3 moves
4. HARD to EASY in 4 moves
5. HEAT to COLD in 4 moves
6. WALK to TROT in 8 moves
7. SILK to RAGS in 5 moves
8. DUST to WASH in 4 moves
9. TAKE to JAIL in 4 moves
10. SLOW to FAST in 6 moves
11. SAIL to SHIP in 4 moves
12. WHITE to BLACK in 8 moves
13. DAWN to DARK in 2 moves
14. MOON to STAR in 6 moves
15. RICH to POOR in 8 moves
16. DRY to WET in 6 moves
17. RAIN to SNOW in 7 moves
18. MOTH to FIRE in 4 moves
19. BIRD to WING in 5 moves
20. HERE to GONE in 5 moves

45

PUNCTUATION PUZZLES

The following sentences look pretty odd in their present form. See if you can punctuate and capitalize them so they will make sense.

1. were but but and and and but but but and and would be and and but
2. I said I said you said I said said he said who said I said you said said I said said is not said like said

46

GUESS THE WORDS

Can you crack all five of these word challenges?

1. What five-letter word beginning with "l" and ending with "d" can mean black-and-blue, ashen gray, or seeing red?
2. What word when spelled forward is quiet but when spelled backward might be a noisy, repeated bar order?
3. Can you make one word out of "new door"?
4. Can you find a seven-letter word whose first two letters refer to a man, first three letters to a woman, first four to a great man, and the whole word to a great woman?
5. What plural word is no longer plural when an "s" is added to the end of it?

47

GEOGRAPHICAL BURIALS

The name of a geographical location is buried in each sentence. One sentence contains both the current and former name of a location.

1. There will be a special sale Monday.
2. I saw the hobo go, taking his pack with him.
3. Jean stole Dorian's gray sweater.
4. He stayed for a week in a spa in the mountains.

5. The necklace was made of beautiful amber links.
6. Grandpa rises before anyone else in the family.
7. There was one cub and two adult lions in the zoo exhibit.
8. Ten boys volunteered to help, but ten others didn't.
9. If his partner slips, what can a dancer do?
10. The mailman said, "Yes, I am not stopped by sleet, hail, and snow."

48

RE-WORD IT

See if you can enter the five words into the spaced lines, reading across, so that seven ordinary words can be read downward. Don't change the order of any of the letters in the five words.

OTTER   ADDER   WATER   TENOR   SENOR

— — — — —

— — — — —

— — — — —

— — — — —

— — — — —

49

WORD CHARADE

In this puzzle poem each line refers to a single letter. The final solution, which is clued in #8, is a word composed of the seven letters reading down.

1. ___ my first is in apple, but not in plum
2. ___ my second in lively, but not in dumb
3. ___ my third is in saves, but not in thrift
4. ___ my fourth is in blow, but not in drift
5. ___ my fifth is in that, but not in this
6. ___ my sixth is in welcome, but not in bliss
7. ___ my seventh is in death, and also in fate
8. my whole is the name of a southern state

50

NUMBERS AND LETTERS

For the first four problems, add a letter to a number (as the number is spelled) to create an answer word. For the last three problems, subtract a letter from a number (as the number is spelled). The positioning of the added or subtracted letter can be anywhere within the number.

For example: what number + what letter = a man's name
Answer: seven + t = Steven

1. what number + what letter = look after
2. what number + what letter = zero
3. what number + what letter = a cake ingredient
4. what number + what letter = scale reading
5. what number – what letter = tied
6. what number – what letter = a Biblical pronoun
7. what number – what letter = animal's covering

51

ANOTHER SPELLING BEE

Start with any letter in the square shown below. Move one square at a time in any direction (including diagonally) until you have spelled out a common English word of four or more letters. You can't revisit the same letter to spell a word. Also, do not use proper names or form plurals by adding "S" to a three-letter word. Par on this is 15 words in 30 minutes. Can you find one 13-letter word?

D	W	I	N	S
E	G	Z	K	G
L	J	Q	U	A
O	W	M	C	P
T	N	K	Y	R

52

DO U KNOW IT?

Can you think of the two words with opposite meanings, both of which start with "u," end with "e," and whose middle letters are the same, although in a different order?

53

NOUN AND VERB

For each of these pairs, come up with a single word that, as a noun, is a synonym for the first word and, as a verb, is a synonym for the second word. For example, "trip" can mean "journey" (noun) and "stumble" (verb).

1. handbag and pucker
2. carton and spar
3. herd and tamp

4. coverlet and toss
5. performance and reveal
6. skin and conceal

54

A WELL-SCRAMBLED PROVERB

And here, to end this section, is one that will please some and cause others to wonder who invents such things. The puzzle is to rearrange the following letters so as to form a well-known and appropriate proverb:

A A A B E E G G H H H H L L L O S S S S T T U U W

End of WORD and LETTER Puzzles

Answers to these puzzles start on page 166

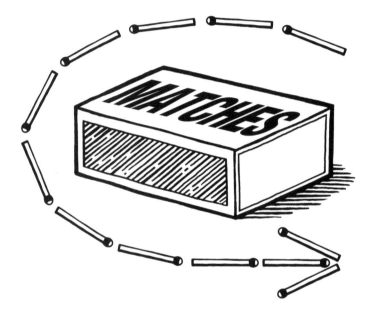

Matchstick PUZZLES

55

WHAT ARE MATCHES MADE OF?

This is one of the oldest match puzzles, but one with which many people nowadays are not acquainted. It also holds an answer that is often unanticipated. Arrange 13 matches on a table as shown to form four squares. The puzzle now is to remove one match and rearrange three others so as to spell the word meaning what matches are made of.

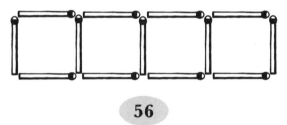

56

THE THREE SQUARES

Cut two matches in half and put them on the table with four other matches so that you have four full-length and four half-length matches. The puzzle is to arrange the eight pieces so that they will form three equal squares.

57

6 PLUS 5 EQUALS 9

The solution to this puzzle may be simple to those who are acquainted with "match mathematics," but it will puzzle a good many others who are not so equipped. Six matches are placed on a table. The problem is to add five matches to the six so as to make nine.

58

FROM 6 TO 3

Arrange 17 matches as shown to form six squares. The puzzle is to remove five matches, not move any others, and end up with three squares, each the same size as the original squares.

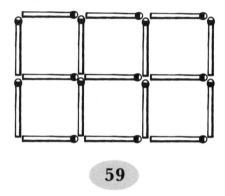

59

FROM 6 TO 2

Again, arrange 17 matches as shown above. Now see if you can remove six matches, not move any others, and end up with two squares. The squares don't both need to be the same size as the originals.

60

FROM 9 TO 2

Arrange 24 matches as shown to form nine squares. See if you can remove eight matches, not move any others, and end up with two squares of any size.

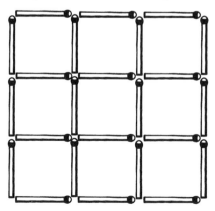

61

THE BRIDGE OF MATCHES

Place four drinking glasses and four matches on a table. The puzzle is to make a bridge by combining the eight items so that it will support a fifth drinking glass. The bridge is to be made by placing the matches on the glasses, but only one end of each match is allowed to rest on a glass.

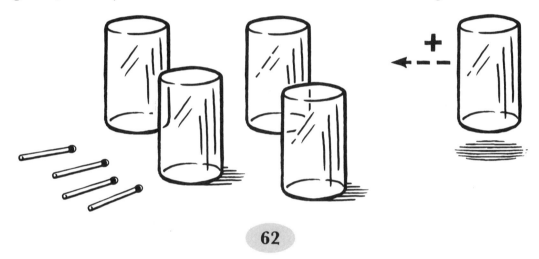

62

FROM FALSE TO TRUE

Arrange seven matches to represent this false equation, two equals six:

The puzzle is to move one match (but neither from the equal sign) and end up with a true mathematical equation. There are two possible solutions.

63

THREE DIFFERENT SHAPES

This is a hard one and will probably require quite a bit of experimenting. Carefully cut the tips off of six matches and place them on the table. Then see if you can arrange them so that the interior spaces between the matches will form two triangles and a two-headed arrow.

64

OVERLAPPING SQUARES

Arrange 12 matches as shown to form four squares. See if you can remove two matches, not move any others, and end up with two overlapping squares of any size.

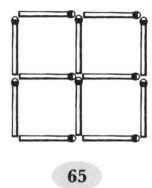

65

TAKE AWAY 2 AND LEAVE 2

Arrange 12 matches as shown to form three squares. Then remove two matches and rearrange the remainder so as to leave two. There's a trick to this and the next two puzzles, so you might want to solve them together.

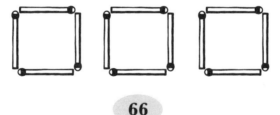

66

TAKE AWAY 3 AND LEAVE 10

Again, arrange 12 matches as shown above to form three squares. Now remove three matches and rearrange the remainders so as to leave ten.

67

TAKE AWAY 1 AND LEAVE 1

Using the same starting arrangement as the two previous puzzles, remove one match and rearrange the remainders so as to leave one.

68

THE 10 PUZZLE

Arrange 15 matches as shown. See if you can remove six matches, not move any others, and end up with ten.

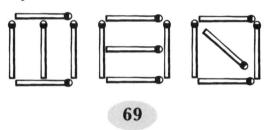

69

THE 10 X 10 PUZZLE

Again, arrange 15 matches as shown above. Now see if you can remove six matches, not move any others, and end up with 100.

70

FOUR TRIANGLES

Put nine matches on the table and see if you can form four equilateral triangles of equal size.

71

BIG AND LITTLE SQUARES

Make a big square as shown using eight matches. Construct a little square inside the big one using four matches. The puzzle is to take the eight matches from the big square and join them to the little square so as to form four squares, each of the same size.

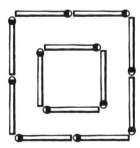

72

FROM 9 TO 5

Arrange 24 matches as shown to form nine squares. See if you can remove four matches, not move any others, and end up with five squares, each of the same size as the original squares.

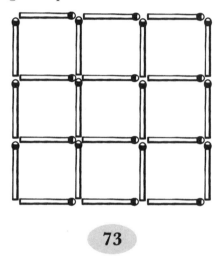

73

FROM 4 TO 2

Arrange 12 matches as shown to form four squares. See if you can rearrange four matches, not move any others, and end up with two squares of any size.

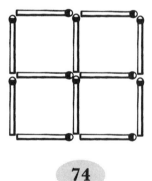

74

MATCH TRIANGLES

Put 12 matches on the table and start to arrange them in the form of triangles, with one match forming each side of each triangle. The puzzle is to make six triangles with the 12 matches.

75

FROM 4 TO 3

Arrange 12 matches as shown to make four squares. Now see if you can rearrange three of the matches, not move any others, and end up with three squares, each of the same size as the originals.

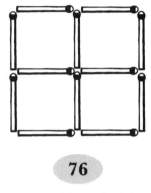

76

5 MAKES 19

Take five matches and, without breaking or bending any of them, see if you can arrange them to form the number 19. One added twist — no part of the arrangement may be more than one match tall.

77

THE TWO DIAMONDS

Take six matches and put them on a table in the form of a hexagon as shown. The puzzle is to rearrange two of the matches in the hexagon, add one extra match, not move any others, and end up with a figure composed of two diamonds.

78

FROM 7 TO 5

Arrange 20 matches as shown to form seven squares. This can be considered as a small office building with seven single-person offices. The firm inhabiting the offices reduces its staff by two employees, however, and it's decided to convert the seven offices into five so that each of the remaining employees can have windows on all four sides. By rearranging only three walls, and leaving the others untouched, see if you can form five offices, each with four outside walls and each of the same size as the originals.

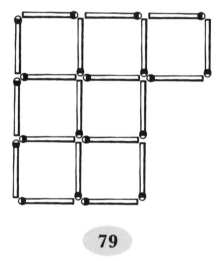

79

FROM 5 TO 4

Here's another building in need of a makeover. First, arrange 16 matches as shown to form five squares, or offices. Now see if you can rearrange three matches, or walls, not move any others, and end up with four offices, each with four outside walls and each of the same size as the originals.

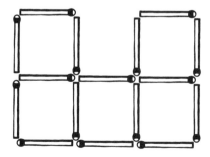

80

THE TRICKY PUZZLE

This is one of the trickiest of all the match rearrangement puzzles, since more shifting is required than usual. Start by arranging 12 matches as shown to form four squares. The problem is to rearrange six matches, not move any others, and end up with three squares of the original size.

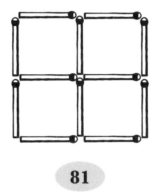

81

THE THREE-MATCH SQUARE

Here's a quick trick to try on a friend. Hand them three matches and ask that they make a square using only the three matches. When they inevitably fail, you proudly boast, "I can make it for you with those three matches! Would you like to see me make it?" How will you accomplish this feat?

82

FROM 8 TO 3

Arrange 22 matches as shown to form eight squares. Then see if you can remove seven matches, not move any others, and end up with three squares of any size.

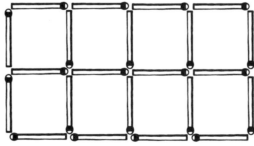

83

THE LAST MATCH

This is a puzzle game to play with an opponent — and always win! Put 17 matches on the table. The two of you must alternate removing matches, never more than three at a time. The point is to keep from picking up the last match. First, see if you can figure out how to always win. Then look in the answer section to see if you're right — or to discover the secret.

84

FROM 5 TO 3

Arrange 15 matches as shown to form five squares. The problem is to remove three matches, not move any others, and end up with three squares, each of the same size as the originals.

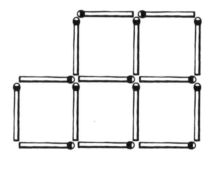

85

GUARDS AND PRISONERS

This is a different kind of match puzzle. Break the heads off three matches and call these the prisoners. Let three unbroken matches represent the guards. Draw a line on a piece of paper to represent a river, and put all six matches to the right of it. The puzzle is to transfer all six prisoners and guards via boat to the other side of the river. There are only two rules:

1. When crossing the river right to left, two passengers must always be in the boat, one of which must bring the boat back.
2. Prisoners can never be unguarded, on either river bank or in the boat.

86

TRIANGLE TROUBLE

Take six matches and see if you can arrange them to form six equal-sized equilateral triangles and one hexagon. As a hint, the arrangement will also form two larger equilateral triangles.

87

TRICKY 20

Here is an honest but tricky match puzzle. The problem is to take five matches and arrange them in such a way that when one of them is removed, you're left with 20.

88

THREE AND A HALF DOZEN

Here's another tricky one, and not well known either. Give a friend nine matches and ask him if he can make three and a half dozen of them without breaking or in any other way changing their size or form. This seems an impossibility, but it is easy if you know how.

89

BING CROSBY'S MATCH PUZZLE

This one was reported to be a favorite of Bing Crosby's. The problem is to arrange six matches in a pattern so that every match touches each of the other five.

90

SQUARES AND TRIANGLES

This is another exceptionally good one. Take eight matches and see if you can arrange them in a figure that contains two squares (one of which is the outline created by the eight matches) and four triangles. All the matches are to lie flat on the table.

91

TRIANGLE BUILDING

This a very good one to try on your friends, because they may have quite a difficult time solving it. The problem is to take six matches of equal length and with them form four equilateral triangles of equal size. Hint: having glue or tape at hand might help greatly in solving this puzzle. Or, if you prefer, try drawing your solution.

92

SQUARE TRIANGLE BUILDING

Like the last puzzle, this one might pose somewhat of a challenge without a bit of adhesive — or a pencil and a piece of paper on which to plot out your solution. The puzzle is to use nine matches to form a figure composed of three equal squares and two equal triangles.

93

THE SWIMMING FISH

Take eight matches and arrange them so as to create an angelfish swimming toward the left. Now see if you can move three matches, not move any others, and turn the fish around so that it's swimming to the right.

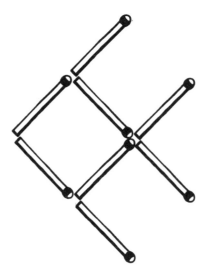

94

NO SQUARES

Arrange 40 matches as shown. Note that the arrangement forms one large square containing 16 smaller squares as well as many other intermediate squares. The puzzle is to remove nine matches, not move any others, and end up with an arrangement that contains no squares of any size.

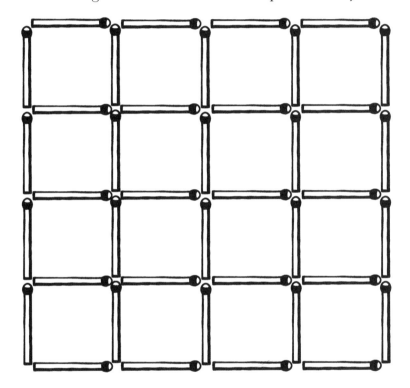

End of MATCHSTICK Puzzles

Answers to these puzzles start on page 173

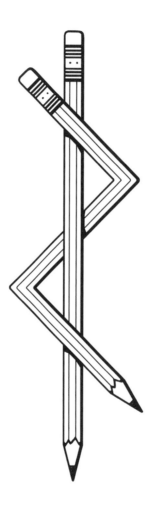

Brain Twister
PUZZLES

95

WEIGHT LIFTING

Using a rope and pulley, Jim was trying to raise a weight from the ground to a platform 25 feet overhead. Each time Jim raised the bottom of the weight ten feet, it slipped back five feet. When the bottom of the weight finally reached the platform, how many total feet had it traveled?

96

THE BAR OF SILVER

A wealthy man, back in the days when paper currency did not circulate freely, had a bar of silver 30 inches long. He agreed to pay an employee hired for the month of April exactly 1/30 of the bar for each of the 30 days. The silver was hard to cut, however. That being the case, what was the smallest number of cuts he could make and yet still be able to keep his new employee paid up to date for each day?

97

DOUBLE, DOUBLE, TOIL AND TROUBLE

Common yeast has some very strange characteristics that are not generally realized. One of these is that in some types of yeast the cells double every minute, with the maximum number of cells being reached one hour after starting with a single cell. That is all very simple and straightforward. However, how long would it take for the maximum number of cells to be reached if one were to start with two cells?

98

HOW MANY HAYSTACKS?

A farmer had a large field with six haystacks in one corner, half as many in another corner, twice as many in another corner, and four in the fourth corner. In piling the hay together in the center of the field, the farmer let one of the stacks get scattered over the field by the wind. How many haystacks did the farmer finally have?

99

THREE CARDS

The backs of three playing cards are shown below. There is at least one three to the right of a two. There is one three just to the left of a three. There is at least one club to the left of a diamond, and there is one club just to the right of a club. See if you can identify the three cards.

100

WHAT'S YOUR NAME?

One day Mr. Jones got off the train in Chicago and, while passing through the station, met an old friend he had not seen in years. With his friend was a little girl.

"Well, I certainly am glad to see you," Mr. Jones said to his friend.

"Same here," replied his friend. "Since I last saw you, I've gotten married — to someone you never knew. This is my little girl."

"I'm so glad to meet you," Mr. Jones said to the little girl. "And what's your name?"

"It's the same as my mother's," answered the little girl.

"Oh, then your name is Anne," said Mr. Jones. How did he know?

101

WHICH IS HEAVIER?

Which is heavier, a pound of feathers or a pound of gold? Go easy, there's more to this than meets the eye.

102

THREE SMALL BOYS

Three small boys were talking together when they were joined by an older man. The newcomer noticed that each of the three boys had a smudge of dirt on his forehead.

"Boys," he said, "each of you look at the foreheads of the other two and, if you see a smudge of dirt on either or both, raise your hand." All three boys looked, and all three raised their hands.

"Now," said the man after they'd lowered their hands, "if one of you is certain that he has dirt on his own forehead and can tell me how and why he knows this, he is to raise his hand and I will give him a quarter."

The three boys looked at each other for a few moments, and then one of them raised his hand. Can you figure out how he knew that he had a smudge on his forehead?

103

THE PAYCHECK PUZZLE

Mrs. Brown gave her gardener a check in full payment for some extra work. The check was for three figures (no cents), with each of the numbers being larger than the one directly preceding it.

"Just a minute," said Mrs. Brown. "If you will rip up the check, I will pay you in cash the difference between *the product* of the three figures on the check and *the sum* of those figures. I can tell you that this is not a small number."

The gardener immediately agreed to this apparently generous offer but was soon gravely disappointed. The cash total turned out to be *nothing*, which, as the artful Mrs. Brown had promised, was not a small number. How much was the check made out for?

104

WHAT HAPPENED TO THE DOLLAR?

Three men stopped at a hotel one night and went to three separate rooms. The charge for the rooms was $10 each, so the men paid a total of $30. The next day the desk clerk was told that the three rooms could be rented for a package rate of $25 instead of the $30 paid. Accordingly, he gave the bellboy five one-dollar bills to return to the three men.

As it happened, the bellboy was not entirely honest, so he gave each of the three men a single dollar and kept the remaining two for himself. Now each man, after receiving the $1 rebate, had paid only $9 for his room. That made $27 for all three. Since the bellboy kept the other $2, which makes $29, what happened to the other dollar?

105

WHAT DAY?

A man went to town one day with $50. After buying pork chops at the meat market and having his eyes tested for glasses, he returned home with $150.

Now, this man's only source of money was his weekly Thursday paycheck, and the only place to cash it was at the town's bank, which was only open on Tuesday, Friday, and Saturday. The eye doctor doesn't keep office hours on Saturday, and the meat market is closed on Thursday and Friday. What day did the man go to town?

106

TWELVE MEN AND ELEVEN ROOMS

Twelve men came to a hotel one night, unfortunately to discover that it had only 11 vacant rooms. The desk clerk thought the matter over for a minute. He then said to the first man: "Mr. Smith, if you will stay here, I will show the others to their rooms. Then I will take care of you."

He put the second man in the first room, the third man in the second room, and so on until the eleventh man was in the tenth room. Then he returned to Mr. Smith and said: "Just step this way, please. I will put you in the eleventh room." Figure out what happened.

107

WHO'S WHO ON THE BALL TEAM?

Using a bit of reasoning, you should be able to figure out the position of each of these men on a baseball team: Bill, Bob, Ed, Frank, Harry, Jack, Jim, Joe, and Tom. Their nine positions are: pitcher, catcher, four infielders (first base, second base, shortstop, third base), and three outfielders (left, center, right). Familiarity with baseball isn't necessary for solving this puzzle.

1. Joe and the third baseman live in the same building.
2. Bob, Joe, Frank, and the catcher were once beaten at golf by the second baseman.
3. Either Tom or Ed is an outfielder, but not both.
4. The shortstop, the third baseman, and Frank each like to go to the races.
5. Bill and Jack married the second baseman's two sisters.
6. Bob and Harry often beat the pitcher at horseshoes.
7. Among the pitcher, catcher, and infielders, only Harry, Joe, and Ed have been with the team for more than five years.
8. The pitcher married Frank's sister.
9. Bill and the three outfielders often play gin rummy together. Bob sometimes watches.
10. Ed is a very close friend of the catcher.
11. Jack and Frank each weigh more than the first baseman.
12. Joe, Bob, Ed, and the shortstop are teetotalers.
13. The four infielders often eat out with Joe and Harry.
14. Jack and the center fielder are best friends.
15. Ed used to play both first and second base.
16. Tom likes to hang out at both the center and left fielder's houses.

108

WHAT A FAMILY

There is an equal number of sons and daughters in the Robinson family. If another son was born, each daughter would have three times as many brothers as sisters. How many sons and daughters are there now?

109

NOON AND SUNSET

In a city in California the sun is more than a thousand miles nearer the earth at noon than it is in the evening when it sets. Can you figure out why this is?

110

EGG BOILING

This one may sound simple, but it has fooled plenty of people:

If it takes three minutes to boil an egg, how many minutes does it take to boil three eggs?

111

WHAT KIND OF BILLS?

One day a woman opened a drawer she hadn't looked in in years and discovered six old bills, none of which were $1 bills. The total sum of the bills was $63. Can you figure out their denominations?

112

WHO'S THE OFFICER?

An army patrol captured three prisoners, all in ragged clothes and without identifying marks. Convinced that one of them was an officer and two were his privates, the sergeant of the patrol went about trying to determine who the officer was. He knew from past experience that the officer would be sure to lie. He also knew that the privates probably wouldn't lie.

The first prisoner he questioned murmured some guttural words and fainted. The second prisoner pointed to the first and said, "He said he's a private. That's true, both he and I are privates."

The third prisoner pointed at the second and said, "He's a liar."

Despite the prisoners' statements, the sergeant soon figured out who was the officer and which two were his privates. How did he do it?

113

THE SIGNPOST

A hiker arrived one rainy night at a spot where three paths met. Looking anxiously for the signpost that would tell him which path to take to his destination, he saw that it had fallen into some nearby bushes. Picking it up, and with little need to think about it, he put it back up and continued on the correct path. How do you think he managed this?

114

FAMILY PARTY

One Christmas there was a fine family party of ten people, which included two grandfathers, two grandmothers, three fathers, three mothers, three sons, three daughters, two mothers-in-law, two fathers-in-law, one son-in-law, one daughter-in-law, two brothers, and two sisters. How was this possible?

115

ALONE, ALONE, ALL ALL ALONE

A young man, otherwise quite sane, once said: "I had luncheon today with my father's mother-in-law's husband, my stepbrother's nephew's father, and my stepmother's father-in-law. Yet I ate by myself." How do you think this was possible?

116

HOW MANY SPARES?

Two friends were about to start an 18,000-mile automobile trip. "Well," said one, "our tires have just been checked and the garage man says each of them is good for 12,000 miles, but not a foot farther. How many spares will we need to do the full 18,000 miles?"

His friend mulled this over for a moment or two and then came up with the right answer. Can you figure the minimum number of spare tires they would need?

117

THE ANT'S PATH

Imagine a room that is 30 feet long, 12 feet wide, and 12 feet high such as is shown in the perspective drawing below.

Now imagine an ant positioned on the center line of the right wall at a point just one foot below the ceiling. On the center line of the left wall exactly one foot above the floor is a splotch of honey.

The ant naturally wants to get to the honey as fast as it can. What is the shortest possible route it can take crawling along the surfaces? How long is that route?

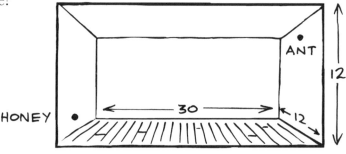

118

THE LEAKY BAG

One day, needing to make a few purchases, a woman dipped into the stash of dollar bills beneath her mattress. Not being able to locate her purse, she stuffed the cash into a paper bag and headed to the store — unaware that the bag had a big hole in it.

A single dollar bill fell from the bag as she entered the store. She then used half of the money remaining in her bag for a small lamp. Two more dollar bills fluttered to the floor as she made her way to the framing department. Once there, she then used half of her remaining money for a small frame. Two more dollars again found their way out of her bag before she spent half of what she then had for some pincushions. Finally, another two dollars were lost before spending half of her remaining money for a nail file. Her very last dollar fell to the pavement as she exited the store.

How much money did she have when she started out, and how much did she spend for each of the things she bought?

119

AN ODD MARRIAGE

There was a wedding one day recently that had the following results: The father of a young woman became her husband's brother-in-law, and her husband's sister became her stepmother. How did this happen?

120

WHO HAS HOW MUCH?

Mrs. Jones has more money than Mrs. Brown. Mrs. Brown has more money than Mrs. Rose. Mrs. Carr has less money than both Mrs. Jones and Mrs. Brown, but more money than Mrs. Rose. Only Mrs. Stevens has more money than Mrs. Smith. If the poorest of them has $1,500 and any differences in wealth are in increments of $1,500, how much does each have?

121

THE SIX COLLEGE MEN

Bob, John, Sam, Rich, Harry, and Martin each go to one of the following six colleges: Harvard, Yale, Princeton, Columbia, Dartmouth, or Cornell. Given the following statements, see if you can figure out which college each man attends:

1. Bob's girlfriend is Julie.
2. John's girlfriend is Regina.
3. Sam's girlfriend is Clara.
4. Rich's girlfriend is Sarah.
5. Martin's girlfriend is Debby.
6. Clara doesn't know any Cornell men.
7. Debby never met any Columbia men.
8. Sarah doesn't date a Harvard man.
9. Norah dates one of the six men.
10. Julie dates only Yale or Darmouth men.
11. Debby and Norah won't date Princeton men.
12. John has a "Y" on his football sweater.

122

WHAT COLOR WAS THE BEAR?

Four men set up camp in the wilderness. Starting from their camp the next day, they walked ten miles due south, and then ten miles due west, where they came across a set of bear tracks. In the distance they saw a bear and hightailed it back to their camp, a jaunt of exactly ten miles. What color do you think the bear was?

123

DINNER OUT

Six women named Hall, Bates, Hicks, Morris, Grant, and Conway met for dinner one evening while their husbands were out bowling. They sat around a circular table at the local fish house. Given the set of facts below, see if you can identify where each woman sat and what color dress she was wearing: brown, cyan, flowered, lime green, mauve, or silver.

1. The woman in the mauve dress sat directly opposite Mrs. Grant.
2. The woman in the silver dress sat opposite Mrs. Bates.
3. Mrs. Bates sat between the brown and the mauve dress wearers.
4. The flowered dress wearer sat opposite Mrs. Hicks, next to the silver dress wearer, and on the mauve dress wearer's right.
5. Mrs. Hall sat next to Mrs. Grant and opposite the woman wearing the lime green dress.
6. Mrs. Morris sat opposite the woman in the cyan dress.

124

FUNNY TRAVELER

Bill travels 45.5 miles every day. In his travels he doesn't notice any traffic lights and he never passes any streets, automobiles, trees, fields, rivers, or houses. He doesn't fly, walk, run, swim, travel on any animal, navigate by boat, or ride in any vehicle that runs on tires. He is not alone in his travels, for he has many fellow travelers who do the same as he does. How does Bill do this?

125

TARGET PRACTICE

Shown below is a strangely numbered archery target. One day an archer was practicing and made a score of exactly 100. How many arrows were used and where did they land?

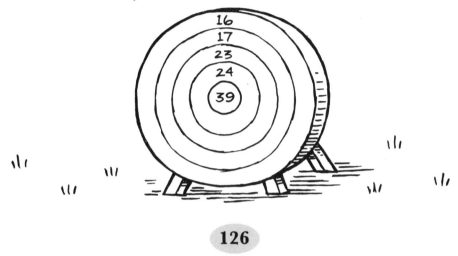

126

WINE AND WATER

There are two glasses of the same size and shape, one containing water and the other wine. A woman takes a spoon and transfers a spoonful of water from the water glass to the wine glass. Then she takes a spoonful of the mixture from the wine glass and puts it into the water glass. Now, was there more wine in the water glass or more water in the wine glass?

127

HOW FAR TO DUNHAM?

A man who lived in the village of Dedham had an appointment one day with a friend who lived in Dunham. He planned to start from Dedham at noon and ride his bicycle. Before leaving, he figured that if he rode 15 miles an hour he would reach Dunham an hour too soon, but if he rode 10 miles an hour he would arrive an hour too late.

What is the distance between Dedham and Dunham, and at what speed did the man ride to make his appointment on the dot?

128

HOW OLD IS JANE?

The ages of Jane and Mary when added together make 44 years. Jane is twice as old as Mary was when Jane was half as old as Mary will be when Mary is three times as old as Jane was when Jane was three times as old as Mary. How old, then, is Jane?

129

BUSHELS OF APPLES

A farmer went to the city one day with many bushels of apples to sell. The first customer bought half of the apples and, for some reason best known to himself, half an apple. The second customer bought half of the apples that were left plus half an apple. Likewise, the third customer bought half of what was left and half an apple. The farmer then had just three dozen apples left.

All the apples were whole when he started, all of them remained that way before selling them to the customers, and those that were left were whole. How many apples did he have when he started out?

130

THE THREE DOORS

There are three doors to a house and three women who wish to pass through them. They all enter at the same time, and no two women pass through the same door together. How many possible ways are there for them to enter the house this way, each using a different door?

131

WHO'S THAT MAN?

Here's a classic puzzle that has confused millions and continues to do so. To whom is the speaker referring as "that man"?

Sisters and brothers have I none, but that man's father is my father's son.

132

RISING TIDE

A rope ladder ten feet long is hanging over the side of a ship. The rungs are one foot apart, and the bottom rung is resting on the surface of the water. The tide rises at the rate of six inches an hour. When will the first three rungs be covered with water?

133

THE LYING ARCHEOLOGIST

There was once an archeologist who said that he had found a bronze coin marked 649 B.C. People believed him at first but soon discovered that he must have been telling a falsehood. How did they know this?

134

THE NUTS AND BOLTS JOB

Two young men once applied for a job with a big nuts and bolts manufacturer. Their qualifications were about equal, and it was very hard to choose between them. Finally, the man who was interviewing them made this offer: "The salary for the position is $15,000. I'll give you two options: 1. having your salary raised $3,000 every year; or 2. having your salary raised $750 every six months."

Each of the men picked a different option. Given that the interviewer would like to save his company money, which applicant should he pick?

135

THE TWO "OUT" PROVERB

While teaching English to some foreign students, a professor wrote a well-known six-word proverb on the blackboard. The first and fourth words in it were both "out." He then asked the class if anyone could restate the proverb in two words. One student, who was not completely cured of her broken English habits, raised her hand and said, "Unseen Idiot." What was the proverb?

136

THE PICNIC

Two mothers and two daughters attended a picnic together. The main courses were hot dogs, hamburgers, and grilled chicken — and yet each made a different choice. How could this be?

137

THE TWO COINS

Mr. Brown says to Mr. Green: "I have in my hand two coins. Together they total 55 cents. One is not a nickel. Can you tell me what the coins are?" See if you can figure it out.

138

THE BRIDGE GAME

Four pairs of husbands and wives, the Allens, Bings, Coles, and Deweys, made up a two-table bridge party. No husband played at the same table as his wife. Mrs. Allen and Mrs. Bing were at different tables. Mr. Cole and Mrs. Allen were partners. The women were equally divided between the tables. Can you figure out what foursome was at each table?

139

THREE TRAVELERS

Three travelers once met at an inn in Persia. Two of them brought their provisions with them, as was the custom of the country, but the third, who came empty-handed, proposed to the others that they should all eat together and he would then pay the value of his portion.

This being agreed to, the first man produced five loaves of bread and the second man three loaves, all of which the three men ate in equal shares. The third man then put down eight pieces of money as the value of his third of the food. The others were satisfied with this but quarreled about the division of the money. An impartial passerby decided correctly how the money should be divided. What was his decision?

140

A BATH FOR THE JINX

The jinx decided to take a bath one day. Unfortunately, two simultaneous disasters threatened to drown him. First, the watertight door to his bathroom became jammed shut. Second, the faucet handle stuck and he couldn't stop the flow of water. The room, which contained only the tub, had no other openings besides the one door. As the water rose, the jinx suddenly had an idea that saved him from drowning. What do you think it was?

141

THE CARPENTER'S PUZZLE

A carpenter wanted to cut a plank, which was six feet long and two foot wide, into two equal pieces. He proceeded to cut it halfway through on each side, and yet found he had two feet still to cut. How could this happen?

142

THE SIX SHOPPERS

Six women named Smith, Jones, Brown, Deeds, Mann, and Gregory all went shopping at a five-story department store one bright May morning. Each went directly to the floor that had the article she wished to buy, and each bought just one article. The things they purchased were: a rug, a book, a dress, a hat, a lamp, and a pair of shoes.

All the women, except Mrs. Smith, entered the elevator together on the ground, or first, floor. Two women, Mrs. Brown and the one who bought the hat, got off at the second floor. One woman got off on the third floor to buy a book. The woman who bought the shoes got off at the fourth floor, leaving Mrs. Gregory all alone to get off at the fifth floor.

The next day Mrs. Jones, who received a dress as a present from one of the women who got off at the second floor, ran into her husband returning the hat one of the other women had bought as a present for him. Now, if rugs are sold on the ground floor, and Mrs. Mann was the fifth person to get out of the elevator, what did each of the women buy and on which floor did they buy it?

143

FOX, DUCK, AND A BAG OF CORN

A man owned a fox, a duck, and a bag of corn. One day he came to the bank of a river where there was a boat large enough to hold only himself and *one* of his possessions. If he left the fox and duck alone, the fox would eat the duck. If he left the duck and the corn alone, the duck would eat the corn. How did he cross the river while keeping all three of his possessions intact?

144

FAMILY MIX-UP

What is the minimum number of people involved in the following phrase:

The widowed wife of a widower

145

THE KIND FATHER'S DEAL

There once was a kind father who had two sons in college and, as kind fathers sometimes do, he bought each of them an automobile. Everything was fine while they were away at college, but when they came home for summer vacation, peace deserted the old homestead.

Both boys had the speed bug, and day after day they raced each other to see whose car was faster. The old man and his wife were driven to distraction, fearing that the lads would break their necks or worse. Finally, he made a brilliant decision. He told the boys that his entire fortune was to go to the son whose car came in last in a 10-mile race to be held the following day. "That will *make* them learn to drive slowly," he told his long-suffering wife.

The two cars lined up for the race, the signal was given, and away they went. Did they drive at a snail's pace, each seeking to be last? Far from it. They both tore off in the greatest burst of speed ever.

Since each son wanted to receive the fortune — why did each still try to beat the other?

146

PICK THE WINNER

A fortuneteller foresaw five facts in her crystal ball one day. They pertained to six horses that would be competing in a race that very afternoon. What horse should the mystic bet on to win the race?

1. Planet finished four lengths behind Star.
2. Star finished three lengths ahead of Sunbeam.
3. Sunbeam finished six lengths behind Moonlight.
4. Moonlight finished one length ahead of Daytime.
5. Swift tied with Star.

147

HOBSON'S CHOICE

An outsider was once captured by a local tribe for intruding on their land. After a little while, the chief of the tribe came to the prisoner and told him the following bad news:

"We have a simple method for dealing with those who choose to cross into our land, and this is it. We will allow you to make one statement. If that statement is false, you must jump off a nearby cliff into the bottomless gorge. If the statement is true, we will instead throw you into the bottomless gorge."

The prisoner's desperation gave him genius. Quickly he made the one statement that would prevent the chief from sentencing him to either fate. What did he say?

148

NO CHANGE

Mrs. Higginbotham counted her change one day and found that she had $1.15. However, she could not make change for any coin up to and including a dollar, that is: a nickel, dime, quarter, 50-cent piece, or dollar. She did not have either a dollar bill or a silver dollar. What coins do you think she had?

149

FAMILY RELATIONSHIPS

Experience has shown that people who are good at family trees enjoy the following types of posers quite a bit, while the average person is often thrown into despair. What relation to you is:

1. your sister-in-law's father-in-law's granddaughter
2. your uncle's father's father's wife
3. your mother's aunt's brother's wife
4. the grandson of the only son of your mother's mother-in-law
5. your brother's mother's stepson's father
6. your sister's son's brother's father
7. your aunt's father's only grandchild
8. your mother's mother's son's son
9. your brother's wife's husband's grandfather's wife
10. your nephew's father's father's wife
11. your sister's father's stepson's mother

150

THE PAWN SHOP SWAP

Mr. Higgins owed Mr. Peters $10 but had only $7 with which to settle up. He was a pretty puzzled man but finally had what he thought was a bright idea. He took a $5 bill to a pawn shop and, in a rather odd arrangement, obtained a $4 loan for it. Next, he took the pawn ticket to his friend Mr. Sniggers, who, knowing that the ticket represented $5 in currency, purchased it for $4. Now Mr. Higgins had the necessary $10 to pay his debt. The question is, who lost in the various transactions?

151

TOO MANY GIRLS

A party was attended by a certain number of boy-girl couples and five girls who came alone. The hostess divided them into groups of three, with two girls and one boy in each. How many boy-girl couples had shown up?

152

A TANGLED DEAL

Betty Jones owed Tammy Smith 40 cents, but couldn't dig up this enormous sum. In settlement Tammy said she would pay 60 cents to Betty for a vase that was actually worth more. She gave Betty 20 cents and considered that she was even. Later, however, Tammy discovered that Betty had snitched the vase from little Tilly Tuller, and she had to give Tilly the full value of it, which was 75 cents. Since Tammy was not reimbursed for her loss by Betty Jones, how much do you think she actually lost?

153

THE HORSE THIEF

This one will show how good a detective you are. Four men, Jim, John, Jack, and Joseph, set off one day by horseback for a weeklong camping trip Jim had arranged. Unfortunately, a quarrel soon sprang up between two of the men. That first evening, one of the quarrelers put a bridle and reins on the horse belonging to the man who had offended him, mounted his own horse, and left with both the animals.

The next morning the two campers still possessing horses set out to try to retrieve their companion's. On their way, the local sheriff happened upon the duo and was quite distressed to hear what had occurred. Horse thievery was taken quite seriously in his jurisdiction. Reading the facts below, can you determine the identity of the horse thief and his victim?

1. John wouldn't expose his brother's guilt when they ran into the sheriff.
2. Joseph had arrived from out of town the morning the foursome set off on the trip.
3. Joseph and Jack had met John only five days before the trip.
4. Jack had met Jim's father only once.
5. The man who arranged the camping trip was willing to give evidence against the thief, whom he disliked.
6. The night before the trip, the man whose horse was taken had eaten at a local diner with one of the other campers. His dinner companion did not customarily play golf with John.

154

THE MYSTERIOUS ORDER

At dawn on June 15, during World War II, a Sad Sack soldier was relieved as sentinel after a ten-hour shift. His buddy, Willy, took over his post as he readied himself for leave. Upon passing his captain, the Sad Sack remarked, "Well, Sir, late last night I dreamed we weren't going to win this war, and my dreams always seem to come true."

"Bah!" said the captain, "We've got to win, and we're going to win! For once you're wrong." As the soldier made his way to the front gate, however, the captain suddenly called out to one of the guards stationed there. "Stop that soldier and throw him in the brig!"

Why did the captain do this?

155

THE CUBES

This is a different kind of brain twister that calls for mental picture-forming. Visualize one wooden three-inch cube painted black and then see if you can answer these questions:

1. How many cuts are needed to divide the cube into one-inch cubes?
2. How many one-inch cubes would you then have?
3. How many cubes have four black sides?
4. How many cubes have three black sides?
5. How many cubes have two black sides?
6. How many cubes have one black side?
7. How many cubes are unpainted?

156

BIG AND LITTLE CLIMBER

A big mountain climber and a little mountain climber stood on a cliff. The little mountain climber was the big mountain climber's son, but the big mountain climber wasn't the little mountain climber's father. How is this possible?

157

DROPS OF WATER

During a rainstorm a leak developed in the roof of a farmhouse, so the farmer put a glass directly under it to catch the water. Things started out calmly with only two drops of water falling into the glass during the first hour, but as the storm's fury increased, so too did the number of drops landing in it. Four drops fell during the second hour and six fell in the third. The drops kept on in this way every hour, with the number increasing by two over the number in the hour directly preceding it. At the end of the 10th hour, the glass was filled to the brim.

The question is, during what hour did the glass become half full?

158

THE CHECKERS TOURNAMENT

Four men named Jim Black, John Black, Bob White, and Rob Roy once competed in a checkers tournament. See if you can tell from the following clues in what order they finished:

1. The Black brothers had been college football stars.
2. Bob White beat Rob Roy.
3. The man who finished third said to the winner, "I'm very glad to have met you. I've always heard how skillful you are at checkers."
4. The runner-up was unmarried and had never progressed beyond the fifth grade.
5. Jim Black had caused a good deal of talk when he was an usher at Rob Roy's wedding. He drank too much champagne and proposed to the bride's mother.

159

LINES AND SQUARES

This one is meant to be done without using pencil and paper. Visualize four evenly spaced horizontal lines that are all crossed perpendicularly by four vertical lines spaced in the same way. How many squares are formed?

160

LINK BY LINK

A hard-pressed widow named Beatrice arranged with her landlady to pay her rent with the links of a gold bracelet for one week. The bracelet had seven links, but Beatrice devised a way to cut just one link one time and still be able to give her landlady one link a day each day for the week. How did she pay her rent in the way described?

161

THE HUNDRED COINS

A woman who had the habit of putting coins in a box for savings decided to count up how much she had one day. She found that she had exactly 100 coins with a total value of $5.00. Can you figure out what coins they were and how many of each kind? The coins available to her were pennies, nickels, dimes, quarters, and 50-cent pieces.

162

CUT THE PIE

An entire apple pie is in its tin. Without removing it, can you figure out a way to cut it into eight pieces by making only three cuts?

163

WHO WAS THE PICCOLO PLAYER?

Three men known as Big Bill, Big Bob, and Big Ben had sons who were similarly dubbed Little Bill, Little Bob, and Little Ben. One of these boys played the piano, one the violin, and the other the piccolo. From the following clues, see if you can tell which was the piccolo player.

1. The piccolo player liked to play ball with his father.
2. Little Bill didn't like the piano player.
3. The pianist's father pitched horseshoes every Saturday with a friend.
4. Big Bob never played games or sports.

164

MORE FAMILY RELATIONSHIPS

What relation is William, who has no brothers and sisters, to Walter, if Walter's grandfather is William's father's son?

165

THE POKER PLAYERS

At the end of a small stakes poker game it was found that Bill had lost $4.85 while Jim, Harry, and Walter had respectively won $2.80, $1.40, and 65 cents. They'd been playing with poker chips, but when they tried to settle, they found that it was not so easy. Bill had only a $5 bill and a dime. Jim had a $1 bill, a 50-cent piece, and a quarter. Harry had two $2 bills, a 50-cent piece, and a nickel. Walter had a 50-cent piece, a quarter and a dime.

After a good deal of figuring, Bill and Walter went home all paid up while Jim and Harry finished settling with each other. In the final transaction, Jim paid Harry. How did these lads settle up with each other?

166

FILLING THE PEACH BASKET

A group of workers are picking peaches and putting them into a large basket. They work at such a speed that the number of peaches in the basket doubles every minute. If the basket takes only six minutes to fill, when do you think it was half full?

167

A TWISTER TO END ALL TWISTERS

This one is guaranteed to make even the mightiest intellect reel. The question is:

What is today if, when the day after tomorrow is yesterday, today will be as far from Tuesday as today was from Tuesday when the day before yesterday was tomorrow?

168

TUG OF WAR

Two teams, White and Black, agreed to a tug of war. The rule was that as soon as a single man on one side had been pulled over the center line, the other team would be the winner.

As things got under way, the White team began to slowly gain the advantage, pulling the Black team forward three inches one minute, only to cede two of those inches in the next minute. Given that the nearest man on the Black team started 20 inches from the center line and that things continued at this rate, during which minute would the first man on the Black team be pulled over the line?

169

THE CLOCK'S HANDS

Starting at 30 minutes past midnight and ending 12 hours later, how many times will the hands of a clock cross each other?

170

THE THREE VERSATILE MEN

This puzzle is about three men whose names were Harold, Henry, and Herbert. Each of these men was involved in two of these occupations: banker, lawyer, merchant, painter, writer, and musician. From the clues given below, see if you can figure out in what two occupations each man is engaged.

1. The banker offended the merchant by laughing at his way of doing business.
2. Both the merchant and the writer used to play golf with Harold.
3. The painter got some legal advice from the lawyer.
4. The banker was sweet on the painter's sister.
5. Henry owed the writer $1.00.
6. Herbert beat both Henry and the painter at gin rummy whenever they played together.

171

A FINGER IN THE WATER

A glass of water is placed on a postage scale able to detect fairly small weights. If a finger is gently put two inches into the water without touching the glass, will the scale reading be a greater amount, a lesser amount, or exactly the same?

End of BRAIN TWISTER Puzzles

Answers to these puzzles start on page 180

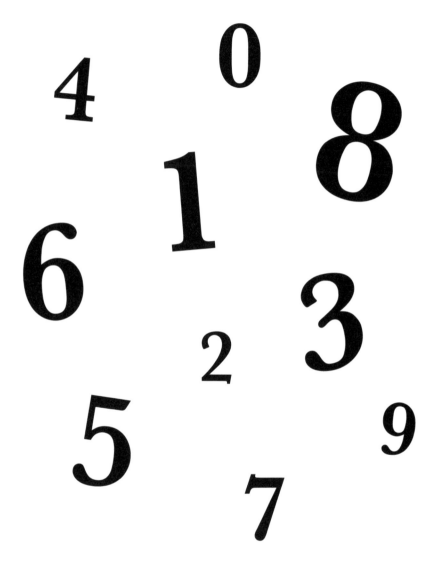

Number ----------- PUZZLES

172

MULTIPLE MIX-UP

This is a good one to try on your friends. Ask someone to write down the number 142,857 and then to multiply it by any number from one to six. When this has been done, ask your friend to tell you any one number in the result. For example, your friend could reply that the fourth number is a five. You can then immediately write down your friend's entire result as well as the multiplying number that was picked. See if you can figure out how to perform the trick. An explanation is given on the answer page.

173

THE NINES PUZZLE

This seems simple but has tripped up many a clever sort:

How many 9's are there between 1 and 100?

174

FROM 45 TO 100

Shown below is a consecutive string of numbers that adds up to 45. The puzzle is to change one plus sign to a multiplication sign so that the problem equals 100. (You might want to enclose the multiplication in parentheses to more clearly indicate that it is performed separately from the additions.)

$$1 + 2 + 3 + 4 + 5 + 6 + 7 + 8 + 9 = 45$$

175

A NUMBER ENIGMA

This has a twist to it, so watch your step. The result will express the most important factor in human happiness.

First, write down a zero. Next, put 50 at its left and five at its right. Finally add one-fifth of eight at its end.

176

FUNNY DIVISION

Try to figure out a way by which you can prove that seven is one-half of 12. This is easier if you are aware of a common trick used in number puzzles.

177

HOW MANY NUMBERS?

Here's a good, straightforward puzzle. How many different 3-digit numbers can be made from the digits 1, 2, and 3?

178

NINE-DIGIT NUMBERS

This is part puzzle and part demonstration. First, write down the largest 9-digit number you can think of that uses each of the digits 1–9 only once. Next, directly under that, write the smallest 9-digit number you can think of that uses each of the digits 1–9 only once. After subtracting the second number from the first one, do you notice anything unique about the answer?

179

THE FOUR PUZZLE

What number, when divided by four, gives the same result as when four is subtracted from it? (Hint: the number is below ten and contains a fraction.)

180

FIND THE NUMBER

This is a fairly difficult problem, but it doesn't require the skills of a mathematician to solve it. Experimenting with the possible numbers, of which there aren't too many, will eventually reveal the correct answer. The puzzle is to find an even number between 100 and 150 that is equal to one-half the sum of all the smaller numbers that divide into it exactly. First pick an even number, and then list all the smaller numbers that divide into it (including 1). When these smaller numbers are added together, their sum should be exactly twice as great as the number chosen.

181

ANOTHER OF THE SAME KIND

Like the previous puzzle, the goal here is to find an even number, this time in the 600's, that is equal to one-half the sum of all the smaller numbers that divide into it exactly.

182

TWICE AND THRICE

Here's a very interesting challenge that can be worked out using both skill and patience. The puzzle is to group the digits 1–9 into three 3-digit numbers. The second 3-digit number must be twice the first 3-digit number. The last 3-digit number must be three times the first 3-digit number. There are actually three ways to do it.

183

ONE ALONE

See if you can create an addition problem composed of two fractions whose sum is exactly one. For example, $2/3 + 1/3 = 1$. There's one added requirement that makes it a bit trickier, though: The two fractions together must make use of each of the ten digits 0–9. Each number is to be used only once in either of the two fractions.

184

FOUR FIVES

Can you combine four 5's so that the value they represent will be 56? Give a little thought as to the different ways numbers can be used and you will probably get the answer in a minute or two.

185

MAGIC MULTIPLICATION

Here's a mathematical demonstration to share with your friends. The results are rather surprising and make one wonder who first discovered them. We've included a blank space below each example for you to see whether the patterns holds up for the next number.

Example 1:

$1 \times 9 + 1 = 10$
$12 \times 9 + 2 = 110$
$123 \times 9 + 3 = 1110$
$1234 \times 9 + 4 = 11110$

Example 2:

$1 \times 9 + 2 = 11$
$12 \times 9 + 3 = 111$
$123 \times 9 + 4 = 1111$
$1234 \times 9 + 5 = 11111$

Example 3:

$1 \times 8 + 1 = 9$
$12 \times 8 + 2 = 98$
$123 \times 8 + 3 = 987$
$1234 \times 8 + 4 = 9876$

_____   _____   _____

186

THE ONE-HALF PUZZLE

Can you create a fraction equal to $1/2$ using each and every one of the nine digits 1–9 exactly once? There are two correct answers.

187

THE ONE-THIRD PUZZLE

Can you create a fraction equal to $1/3$ using each and every one of the nine digits 1–9 exactly once?

188

MISSING NUMBERS

This type of puzzle is one you and your friends can easily create by using different numbers. First, try our three problems, which are solved by finding the missing numbers. To create your own, write down a simple problem and then erase some of the numbers, keeping a record of the erasures. Your friends must then try to reinstate the missing numbers.

Addition:	Multiplication:	Subtraction:
2 9 _	4 8 7 6	8 _ _ 6
7 _ 4 2	x 3 _ 7	- 3 9 8 _
+ _ 2 7 9	———	———
———	1 5 9 4 4 5 2	4 7 7 6
1 0 6 1 3		

189

WHEN SUBTRACTION MEANS ADDITION

See if you can figure out a way to take 1 from 29 and have 30 left. Beware, there's a catch to this one.

190

THE 48 PUZZLE

See if you can find a way to divide the number 48 into two parts so that, when one part is divided by six and the other by three, the sum of those two results will be nine.

191

THE EIGHT 8'S

Using eight 8's, can you create an addition problem that totals 1,000? The 8's all appear as whole numbers — no fractions or decimal points, for example.

192

ADDING AND MULTIPLYING

How much is: 5 + 5 + 5 x 5 x 5 x 5 x 5 x 0?

193

MAGIC SQUARE OF 15

Magic Squares are grid puzzles where the numbers in each horizontal row, in each vertical column, and along each diagonal add up to the same total. A basic Magic Square, such as the one below, contains nine cells into which the numbers 1–9 must be placed, each number being used only once. We've started this one for you. Can you fill in the other six numbers so that the sum of the three numbers in each row, each column, and along each diagonal is 15?

	1	
	5	
	9	

194

MAGIC SQUARE OF 34

Here's a larger Magic Square divided into 16 cells. In this grid, you need to arrange the numbers 1–16 so that the sum of the four numbers in each horizontal row, in each vertical column, and along each diagonal is 34. Again, several numbers have been entered into the grid to get you started.

	2		
		10	
		6	
4			1

195

MAGIC SQUARE OF 65

As the size of our Magic Squares grow, so too does the difficulty. To compensate a bit, we've increased the amount of numbers we've placed into the grid in advance. Your task with this 25-cell grid is to arrange the numbers 1–25 so that the sum of the numbers in each horizontal row, in each vertical column, and along each diagonal is 65.

			8	
23				16
		13		
	12			
			2	9

196

MAGIC SQUARE OF 111

And finally — a Magic Square with 36 cells. Put in the remaining numbers from 1 to 36 so that the sum of the numbers in each horizontal row, in each vertical column, and along each diagonal is 111.

35			26		
		7		23	
	9			27	
		33			15
	5		12		
4					11

197

CROSSED-OUT NUMBERS

Write the following addition problem on a piece of paper:

$$
\begin{array}{r}
111 \\
333 \\
777 \\
+\ 999 \\
\hline
1111
\end{array}
$$

The puzzle now is to cross out some of the numbers so that those remaining will add up to 1,111. To get you started, we'll tell you that two numbers in the 333 line are crossed out, as are two numbers in the 777 line. What, if anything, is to be done in the first and fourth lines we'll leave for you to figure out.

198

THE PHILOSOPHER'S PUPILS

This was a favorite problem among the ancient Greek mathematicians:

A group of admirers once asked: "Tell us, illustrious Pythagoras, how many pupils frequent thy school?"

Pythagoras replied, "One-half study mathematics, one-fourth natural philosophy, one-seventh observe silence, and there are three others besides."

Can you figure out how many students attended Pythagoras's school? In other words, find a number that's equal to its half + its quarter + its seventh + three.

199

THREE PLUS WHAT?

What number, when increased by three and then divided by two, results in a number that is twice itself?

200

THE 33 PUZZLE

This and the next puzzle are variations on the Magic Squares presented on the previous spread. For this puzzle, you must find a way to put the numbers 7–15 into the grid, once each, so that the three horizontal rows, three vertical columns, and two diagonals each add up to 33.

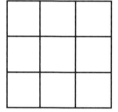

201

THE 1926 PUZZLE

This is the same as the puzzle above except that it uses nine 3-digit numbers. The problem is to put the consecutive numbers 638-646 into the grid, once each, so that the three horizontal rows, three vertical columns, and two diagonals each add up to 1,926. We've widened the grid a bit to allow for the 3-digit numbers. Can you figure out the system for filling a 3 x 3 grid with any set of nine consecutive numbers?

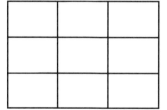

202

ONE HUNDRED EVEN

See if you can create an addition problem that totals 100 using each of the ten digits 0–9 exactly once. The correct problem consists of two 2-digit numbers and two fractions.

203

THE 17 TRIANGLE

Draw a triangle on a piece of paper, with nine dots on its sides as shown. Then see if you can arrange the digits 1–9, one digit next to each dot, so that the four digits on each side add up to 17.

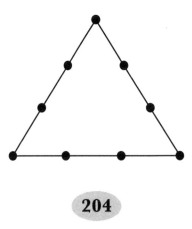

204

THE 20 TRIANGLE

Again, try to arrange the digits 1–9 next to the dots, but this time so that the four digits on each side add up to 20.

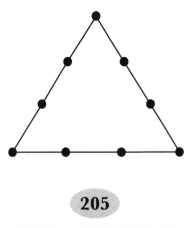

205

THE 24 PUZZLE

Using the same digit three times, can you create a problem whose answer is 24. There are three possible solutions.

206

THE 41 PUZZLE

Here's a very straightforward question, but one that has stumped more than a few solvers:

What two whole numbers, when multiplied together, result in 41?

207

ODD TO EVEN

This puzzle is to take an odd digit and use it exactly three times so that the three digits are equal in value to an even number. Addition, subtraction, multiplication, and division are not used.

208

ONLY FOURS

Using only the digit 4, see if you can figure out a way to express each number from 0–10. You may use as many 4's as you want, but try to find the thriftiest solutions — those that use the fewest 4's. We'll tell you that the fewest total number of 4's needed is 31. Addition, subtraction, multiplication, division, parentheses, and fractions may be used.

209

THE PERFECT QUESTION

A perfect number is one that is equal to the sum of every number that can divide evenly into it, not counting the perfect number itself. For example, $6 = 1 + 2 + 3$. What is the next perfect number after 6?

End of NUMBER Puzzles

Answers to these puzzles start on page 192

In this chapter, when different types of coins are called for, we refer to them simply as white and black coins. You may use whatever you prefer in these cases: two different coins (pennies and nickels, for example), red and black checkers, or poker chips of contrasting colors.

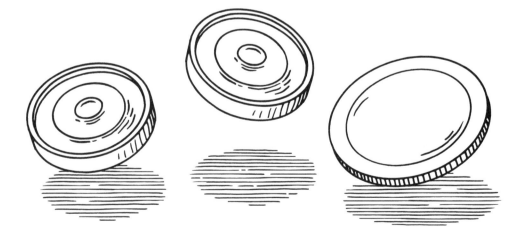

PUZZLES

210

THREE IN A ROW

Here's a simple puzzle to start things off. Or is it? Arrange three coins as shown with one black coin in the middle. Without touching the black coin in any way, can you remove it from its middle position?

211

RIGHT-ANGLE LINES

Arrange six coins as shown. The puzzle is to move one coin so as to make two lines that each contain four coins.

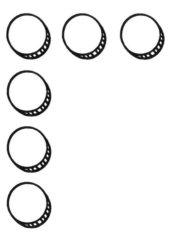

212

MOVE TO THE CENTER

Arrange three coins as shown below. The goal is to get the black coin between the two white coins without breaking these rules:

1. The coin on the left may be moved but not touched in any way. (No blowing the coin or moving the surface its on.)
2. The coin in the middle may be touched but not moved.
3. The black coin may be both touched and moved.

Given these limitations, it sounds impossible. However, it can be done very simply once you know how.

213

MATCHING COINS

Arrange eight white coins and eight black coins in four lines as shown. Note that each horizontal and vertical line contains two coins of each color. The puzzle is to move two black and two white coins to different positions so that the 16 coins will be arranged in four lines, each consisting entirely of either black or white coins. The first line will be all black, the second all white, and so on.

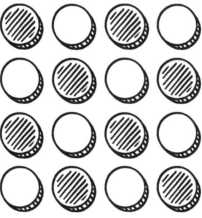

214

STAR POINTS

Draw an eight-pointed star as shown, numbering each point. The puzzle is to cover seven of the star's points with coins in the following manner: Place a coin on any uncovered point and then slide it along one of the two straight lines to an opposite point that is uncovered.

For example, you could start by putting a coin on point 1 and sliding it down to point 6. Point 6 is then covered and may not be used as either a starting or ending point. As you'll quickly discover, covering up seven of the eight points in this way is harder than it might sound.

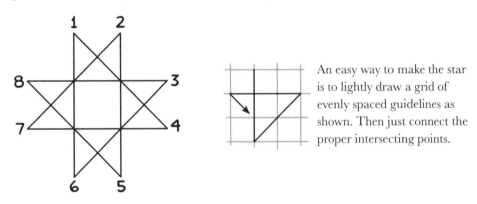

An easy way to make the star is to lightly draw a grid of evenly spaced guidelines as shown. Then just connect the proper intersecting points.

215

ALTERNATE COINS

Arrange four white coins and four black coins alternately in a line as shown in the first illustration. The puzzle is to move any two adjacent coins (together without altering their order) and, in four such moves, group the white and black coins together at opposite ends of the line, as shown in the second illustration.

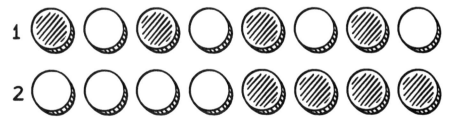

216

FIVE KINGS

Put ten coins in a line as shown below. The goal is make moves until five "kings" have been created (two coins stacked one atop the other). Each move consists of picking any coin, jumping it over two adjacent coins, and then stacking it atop the third coin to make a king (see inset). You can jump in either direction, and jumping over a king counts as jumping over two coins. Empty spaces don't count as coins being jumped over.

217

UPSIDE DOWN

Make a triangle with six coins as shown. Then see if you can turn the triangle upside down — so it points down instead of up — by moving only two of the coins.

218

NINE COINS IN TEN LINES

This is a really hard one, but that makes it all the better to try out on your friends. The puzzle is to arrange nine coins so that they form ten straight lines of three coins each.

219

CHANGING PLACES

Draw a diagram with seven boxes as shown. Place three white coins in boxes 2, 3, and 4 and three black coins in boxes 5, 6, and 7, leaving box 1 vacant. The goal is to reverse the setup so that the black coins fill boxes 1, 2, and 3 and the white coins fill boxes 4, 5, and 6, with box 7 vacant.

To do this, coins are moved one at a time by either sliding them one space into the vacant box or jumping them over one or two other coins to reach the vacant box. A move can be in either direction. The correct solution takes ten moves.

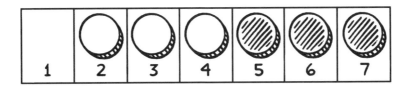

220

MORE CHANGING

Use the same drawing as in the last puzzle, but this time fill the left three boxes with white coins and the right three boxes with black coins, leaving box 4 empty. The goal is to reverse the setup so that the white coins fill boxes 5, 6, and 7 and the black coins fill boxes 1, 2, and 3. Box 4 will again be empty.

Some of the rules for accomplishing this are a bit different from those in the previous puzzle. Coins are to be moved one at a time by sliding them one space into the vacant box or jumping them over *just one* other coin to reach the vacant box. Additionally, the coins can only be moved in the direction of their intended destination — white coins can only move to the right, and black coins only to the left.

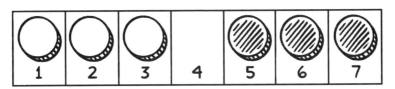

221

TAILS UP

You'll need three coins with heads and tails for this puzzle, arranged as shown. The puzzle is to make three successive moves — the first being to turn over exactly one coin, the second to turn over exactly two coins, and the third to turn over all three coins — so that three tails are then showing.

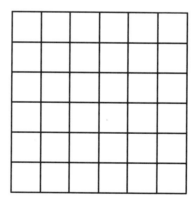

222

DESIGN FOR COINS

Draw a big square divided into 36 smaller squares as shown. Then see if you can place 12 coins into the squares so that they create a design with left-right symmetry (the left half mirrors the right half). There must be exactly two coins in each horizontal row and in each vertical column — but no coins in the two 6-square diagonals crisscrossing the center.

223

TWELVE LINES OF THREE

This one will tax your ingenuity to the utmost. To help a bit, we'll tell you that the solution is a symmetrical geometric shape with a single coin at its center. The puzzle is to arrange 13 coins in 12 lines of three coins each.

224

THE DIAMOND PENDANT

A wealthy lady had 17 very large and beautiful diamonds that she wished a jeweler to mount in a pendant in a very specific way. They were to be arranged so that she could count nine diamonds in six different ways — either in a straight line or in a line that formed a right angle. The jeweler hit upon a way to do this to perfection by using a simple geometric form that is frequently employed for pendants. Using 17 coins as the diamonds, see if you can figure out the arrangement.

225

DOUBLING UP

Draw a circle and inside it twelve small circles numbered 1–12, just like a clock. Then place one coin in each circle. The goal is to make moves until six "kings" have been created (two coins with one coin atop the other), leaving six circles empty. Each move consists of selecting one of the 12 coins, jumping it over two adjacent coins, and landing it atop the third to make a king. The jumps can be made in either a clockwise or counterclockwise direction. Jumping over a king counts as jumping over two coins; vacated circles don't count as coins being jumped over. The correct solution takes six moves.

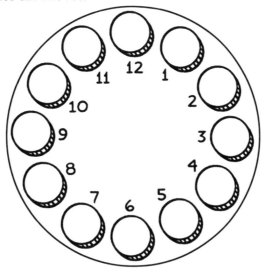

226

FOUR TO A LINE

Put 16 coins on the table and see if you can arrange them so that they form ten straight lines of four coins each. The outline of the solution will form a common shape.

227

COUNT AND TAKE OUT

Draw a circle and inside it ten small circles numbered 1–10. Put white coins in the circles numbered 1, 2, 4, 7, and 9 and black coins in the circles numbered 3, 5, 6, 8, and 10. The goal is to remove all the white coins from the circle, leaving all five black coins untouched.

Coins are removed in the following manner. First, select a number between one and 12. As an example, we'll use 12. Next, select a coin with which to start. We'll use coin 1. Counting this as one, proceed clockwise to the twelfth coin, coin 2. Since coin 2 is white, it's removed — and its vacant spot will not be included in the next count. Now, start a second count from the coin immediately following the removed coin. That will be coin 3. Counting that as one, the twelfth coin will be coin 5. Since coin 5 is black and shouldn't be removed, you must start over. To get you started, we'll advise you that the correct number isn't 12 and coin 1 isn't the correct starting spot.

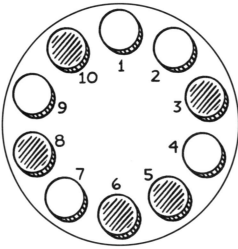

228

HEADS TO TAILS COUNTDOWN

Use your same drawing from the last puzzle, but this time you'll need to use ten coins that have heads and tails. Place the coins in the ten circles so that they all face heads up. The goal is to turn the coins over, in descending order starting with coin 10 and ending with coin 1, so that they all are showing tails.

Coins are turned over in the following manner. First, select a number between one and 12. As an example, we'll use 12. Next, select a coin with which to start. We'll use coin 8. Counting this as one, proceed clockwise to the twelfth coin, coin 10, which is then turned tails up. Now, start a second count from coin 10. A new count of twelve, however, will bring you to coin 2, which is not what you want. The second overturned coin should be coin 9, then coin 8, and so on. Therefore, you must start over choosing another number, another starting coin, or both. Coins already turned over are counted each time.

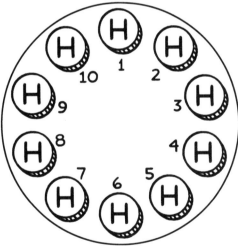

End of COIN Puzzles

Answers to these puzzles start on page 197

An anagram is a word or group of words formed by transposing the letters of another word or series of words. Thus, "time," "item," and "mite" are anagrams of the word "emit."

The construction of anagrams is one of the world's most ancient puzzle pastimes. Anagrams were known to the Greeks and Romans and were popular throughout Europe during the Middle Ages and later, particularly in France. John Dryden, the English poet, called the making of anagrams the "torturing of one poor word ten thousand ways," but many well-known people of his day found great amusement in them.

One of the most famous anagrams is the change of *"Ave Maria, gratia plena, Dominus tecum"* into *"Virgo serena, pia, munda et immaculata."* Others include the transposition of "Horatio Nelson" into "Honor est a Nilo" and of "Florence Nightingale" into "Flit on, cheering angel." The name "Voltaire" is an anagram that the famous French philosopher assumed instead of his family name, Francois Marie Arouet. Voltaire is a transposition of *"Arouet, l.j."* meaning *"Arouet, le jeune,"* or "the younger." In the anagram, "u" becomes "v," and "j" becomes "i."

Anagram
PUZZLES

229

A FEW STRAIGHT ANAGRAMS

Here are some straight or true anagrams, in which the letters of the original phrases have been transposed to form new words that are of common English usage and are related by meaning or implication to the original phrases.

1. Change the anagram NO MORE STARS into a word meaning those who study the stars.
2. Change the anagram IT'S IN CHARITY into a religion.
3. Change the anagram GREAT HELP into an instrument once used in communications that was in fact a great help.
4. Change the anagram BEST IN PRAYER into a religious denomination.
5. Change the anagram GOLDEN LAND into the nickname of a country to which many people think this description applies.

230

A MEAL OF ANAGRAMS

At a dinner party the heading, two appetizers (second line), and two entrees were printed in the form of anagrams. Can you decipher them?

Hum Not, Ingest

Pouter's soy   Steamed root
One solid lamb   Try our steak

231

WORD AND LETTER ANAGRAMS

Word and Letter Anagrams consist of words to which one or more letters are added to form a new word. For example, WORD + C forms the new word CROWD. You can have fun making these up yourself, as well as solving the ones given below. Here are a few that should keep you busy for a few minutes — or possibly longer.

1. ACORN plus:
   ACORN + B
   ACORN + E
   ACORN + H
   ACORN + R

2. More of the SAME:
   SAME + Y
   SAME + H
   SAME + U

3. Ten more good ones:
   TREE + X
   GRAVE + A
   ODOR + P
   VERB + A
   SLAB + T
   RAID + C
   SEVEN + R
   SUITE + Q
   DEIGN + A
   VEAL + G

4. Add two letters:
   ARMY + R and T
   REEF + R and T
   TENSION + A and S

LINK + C and E
REAP + D and A
TREAD + F and G
GRAVE + A and E
DANCE + C and E
SMILE + U and B
CARD + I and N

232

AUTHOR ANAGRAMS

The two anagrams below, when the letters are rearranged, spell the names of two famous authors, one Irish and one English.

I lace words   I'll make a wise phrase

233

STATE ANAGRAMS

In each sentence, rearrange the letters in the capitalized words to spell a state of the United States.

1. HE ordered his MEN to bombard the WARSHIP.
2. The tiger made a DASH after the RED LION.
3. His SON works AT the coal MINE.
4. The NAVY ordered 100 sailors to LINE up on the bridge SPAN.
5. The KEY to the door was very WORN.
6. The dollar gold COIN is A FRAIL one and so is not made anymore.
7. Uncle SAM is SUCH a splendid symbol of the United STATES.
8. The BEAR fell into the canoe and SANK it.

234

AN ANAGRAM DESTINATION

In the 1800s, an Englishman leaving for the Mediterranean wrote a friend that he was going to "plant onions, etc." Can you figure out his destination?

235

ANIMALS, VEGETABLES, AND OTHERS

Transpose the letters in the following anagrams so that they spell, in order, three vegetables, three fruits, three fish, and three jungle animals.

1. a sugar sap
2. a low life cur
3. I hate cork
4. plane pipe
5. one rag
6. ruby rebel
7. elk cream
8. dash
9. rend foul
10. the plane
11. harp net
12. robotic cartons (two words)

236

GEOGRAPHICAL ANAGRAMS

Rearrange the letters in the following anagrams so that they spell, in order, five European countries and five United States cities.

1. near gym
2. laity
3. clan dots
4. or yawn
5. polar tug
6. tried to
7. fringed slip
8. meals
9. casino francs
10. shall eat sea

237

BY LAND AND BY SEA

A famous pair of anagram words are:

CHESTY
CHASTY

See if you can transpose the letters of CHESTY to form a tool used on the land, and transpose CHASTY to form a word describing something used on the sea.

• • • • • • •

"Scrambled Words" are closely related to anagrams. With them, however, the letters of the original words are transposed to form words that have no meaning.

• • • • • • •

238

SCRAMBLED PROVERBS

Here are five well-known proverbs of which each word has been pretty thoroughly scrambled. The word order has been scrambled as well.

1. lafl hegto dripe a ofbeer
2. etim thicts a enni ni vesas
3. kemas stawe shate
4. soms glinrol a notes on tregash
5. mowr yearl het drib teh steg

239

SCRAMBLED POETRY

Here is a perfectly good poem of which the letters in each word have been scrambled so that the whole thing looks like jabberwocky, although the words themselves are still in proper order. See if you can straighten it out.

desibe hte mearsletst ginshin nabd
teh nishefrma tas lal dya.
noso eh dresai a zayl ahdn
ot vired a tnag ayaw.
tey hothug eh was em dinstang yb,
eh vage on douwart sing
tub pekt shi neke and futchwal yee
ponu sih rednels nile.

240

SCRAMBLED EGGS

Rearrange the letters in each of the following to form animals that lay or once laid eggs. The last is an animal of a wholly different sort that has also been known to lay an egg on occasion.

1. ctrohsi
2. kesna
3. ugeninp
4. sitooter
5. staypulp

6. knihcce
7. rykuet
8. naslmo
9. ranidous
10. necodima

241

SCRAMBLED SUBJECTS

Rearrange the letters in each of the following to form a course one might take in school.

1. thyriso
2. globyoi
3. mytegore
4. hgiseln

5. monosecci
6. baelgar
7. naspshi
8. shiscpy

242

SCRAMBLED FAMOUS AMERICANS

Rearrange the letters in each of the following to form twelve famous names from American history.

1. eomrs
2. eeolorstv
3. aehmnrs
4. eiycklmn
5. aiohlmnt
6. dinose

7. eoomnr
8. ouflnt
9. aioghnnstw
10. agnrt
11. ionclln
12. nfosjfree

243

SCRAMBLED STATES

Can you unscramble all the 50 states? Some are easy, but it's a different story with a number of them.

1. regoon
2. saxet
3. mowying
4. nakass
5. waio
6. hodia
7. balamaa
8. kewnroy
9. toamnan
10. zariano
11. sowcinins
12. tremnov
13. hioo
14. weldeara
15. dorfial
16. sarksana
17. ahiawi
18. gashontwin
19. grivaini
20. huat
21. laicairfon
22. rogiage
23. loakmhoa
24. roaldoco
25. nocittuccen
26. veanad
27. namie
28. loinsili
29. kalsaa
30. iiiissssppm
31. shoilaunacort
32. neetsnees
33. grewsainivti
34. danaini
35. kostdouhaat
36. yeckunkt
37. sailunoia
38. isourism
39. bearnsak
40. shirleddoan
41. sylvianannep
42. tokandthoar
43. arthoilcannor
44. dyamlarn
45. wixencome
46. setcashstaums
47. gichmain
48. serjenyew
49. pashwirenhem
50. stoanenim

End of ANAGRAM Puzzles

Answers to these puzzles start on page 202

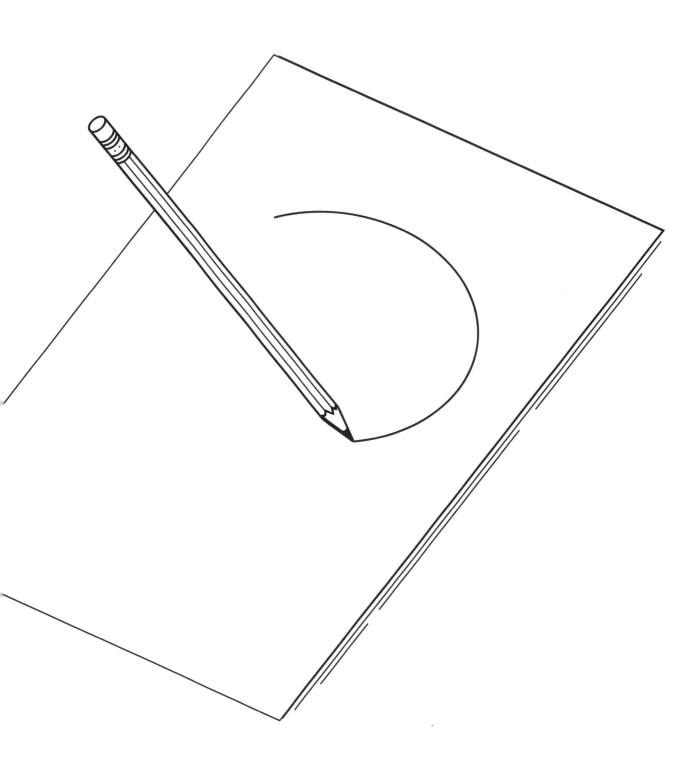

Pencil and Paper
PUZZLES

244
THE OLD KING'S CASTLE

The diagram below represents a bird's-eye view of the old king's castle, with letters marking the spots where guards are stationed. Every night the commander walks a route that visits each guard post exactly once, ending one post away from where he started. The letters along that route also spell out the name of the force that's guarding the castle. Can you find it?

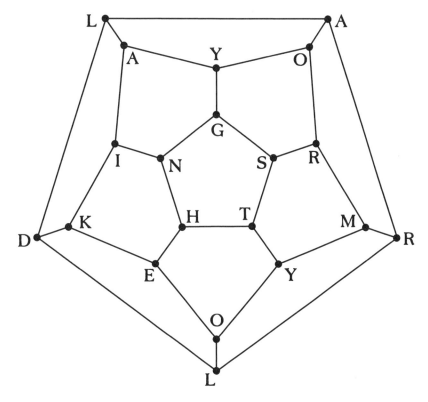

245

THE UNFRIENDLY NEIGHBORS

The people who live in the five houses below are exceptionally unfriendly and don't like to cross each others' paths. This presents a problem since they all leave for work at the same time and their cars are kept in a community garage. The man in house 1 keeps his car in garage 1, the man in house 2 keeps his car in garage 2, and so on. However, there is a way for every man to get to his garage without crossing any of his neighbors' paths. See if you can figure out how to do it.

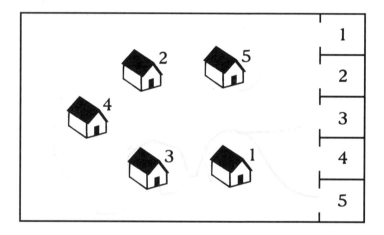

246

THE ONE-LINE ENVELOPE

Shown below is an outline drawing of an envelope with its flap up. Can you draw it in one continuous line without lifting your pencil from the paper and without retracing any line?

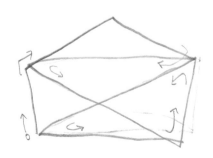
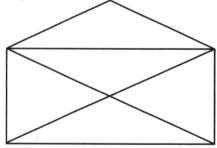

247

WATER, GAS, AND ELECTRICITY

The drawing below shows three newly built houses, as well as the water, gas, and electricity stations to which they need to be connected. See if you can draw lines from all three of the stations to the houses while following one adamant rule: No line may cross another.

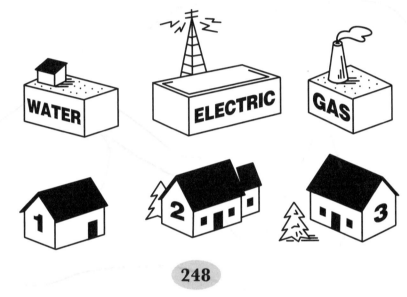

248

FOUR TURNS

The dots in the drawing below represent 14 houses in a neighborhood. One day the mailman decided he wanted to try something different and devised a route that would allow him to visit every house exactly once while walking only in straight lines and changing direction just four times. Make your own drawing and see if you can figure out his new route.

249

THE PLOT OF LAND

Farmer Munson left his four children a plot of land as shown. It was to be divided so that each of them would receive an equal-size plot, each of the same shape as the original. Can you figure out how to do it?

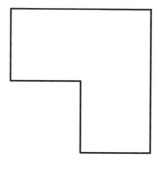

250

A BIGGER PLOT

It turns out Farmer Munson had an even bigger plot, which he wanted leave to his 16 grandchildren. Can you find a way to divide it into 16 equal-sized plots, each of the same shape as the original?

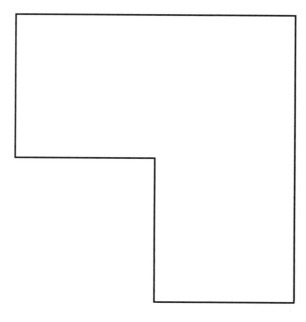

251

PENTAGON TO SQUARE

Draw a pentagon as shown. The proportions should be equal to a square with a right triangle atop it. Then see if you can draw two straight lines across it so as to create three pieces that will fit together to form a square.

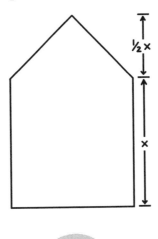

252

SHAPES AND NUMBERS

Draw a square and divide it into 16 smaller squares. Add numbered circles as shown. Now see if you can put the numbered triangles, squares, and diamonds in the remaining 12 spaces so that each horizontal row, each vertical column, and each of the two diagonals contain four different shapes and four different numbers.

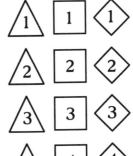

253

SWITCHING THE TRAINS

Two freight trains, each composed of 50 cars and two engines (one at each end), approach from opposite directions. A section of double track sits between them, each half of which will hold 25 cars and one engine. Can you figure out how the trains can be handled so that each can reach the opposite side of the double track and proceed on its way?

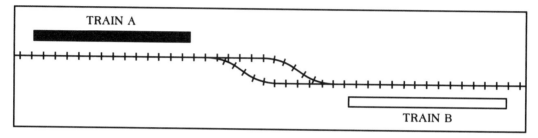

254

DOES 64 EQUAL 65?

This is a simple way to show your friends that 64 equals 65. First draw a square containing 64 smaller squares as shown on the left. Draw the heavy black lines and cut along them with a pair of scissors, dividing the square into four parts. Now put the four parts together to form the rectangle shown on the right. Count the rows of small squares and you'll find that there are five rows of 13 squares each, which totals 65 squares. Can you figure out where the extra square came from?

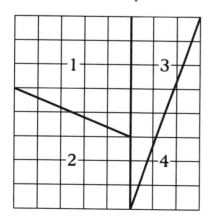
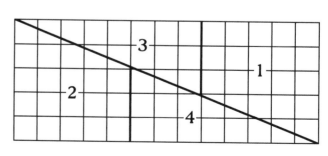

255

FOUR CURIOUS PARTS

Draw a 64-square grid. Write in the letters A, B, C, and D as shown. Now see if you can draw heavier lines along the dividing lines between the squares so that four identical shapes are formed, each of which contains one of the letters.

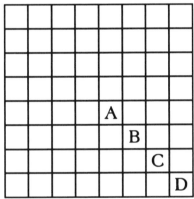

256

AROUND THE SQUARES

Draw the figure below on a piece of paper. Starting at the dot indicated, find a route along the lines that visits each dot exactly once and ends up back at the starting dot. Your route must be a continuous line drawn without lifting your pencil from the paper.

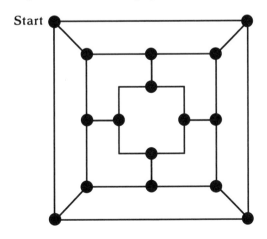

257

TRY-ANGLE

Can you draw the figure below in one continuous line without lifting your pencil or retracing any line? You also can't cross over a line that's already been drawn.

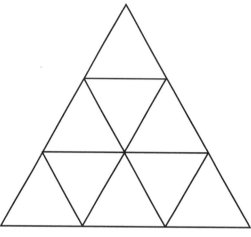

258

DOTS IN THE SQUARE

Draw a square and position 12 dots in it as shown. Then see if you can divide the square into four pieces of equal size and shape, each of which contains three circles.

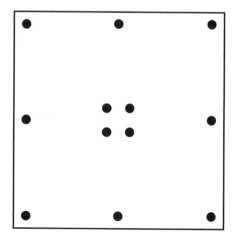

259

THE PIG PEN PUZZLE

A farmer kept his six pigs in a structure made of 19 fence lengths and 14 posts. One day he needed to use seven of the posts and seven of the fence lengths elsewhere. He disassembled the pens, took the posts and fencing he needed, and then found a way to rearrange the remaining 12 fence lengths and seven posts so that all six pigs had a pen, each of an equal size and shape. Can you draw the new arrangement?

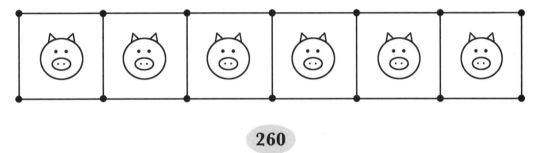

260

THREE GARDEN HOSES

The drawing below shows three water spigots and three vegetable patches in a fenced-in area. See if you can run a hose from spigot 1 to the tomato patch, from spigot 2 to the zucchini, and from spigot 3 to the cucumbers. One rule: The hoses can't cross each other.

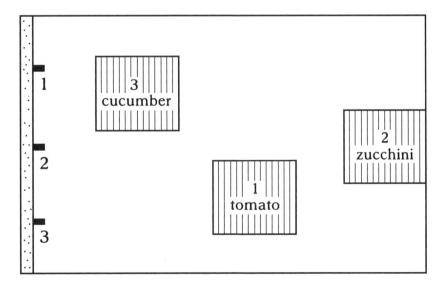

261

A HOLE IN THE BARN FLOOR

There is a hole in a barn floor that is two feet wide and 12 feet long. How can the hole be filled using a board that is three feet wide and eight feet long? It requires cutting the board into only two pieces.

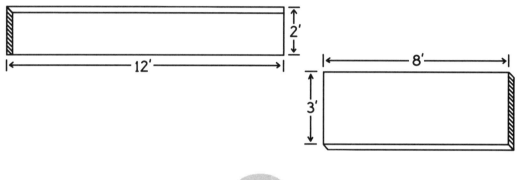

262

STAR AND CIRCLES

Here's another figure you must try to draw in one continuous line without lifting your pencil from the paper. You can't go over the same line twice or cross over a line that has already been drawn.

263

THE FARMER'S FENCE

Mr. Baker had 21 trees in his garden that were arranged symmetrically as shown. One day he decided it would be nice to add some brick edging so that each tree had its own defined bed. He found he could do this by installing eight straight lines of brick, each starting and ending at the garden's border. The right-hand drawing shows his garden after one line was laid. Can you draw in the remaining seven lines?

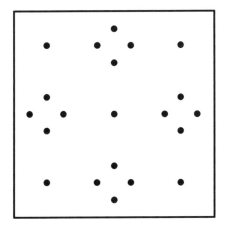 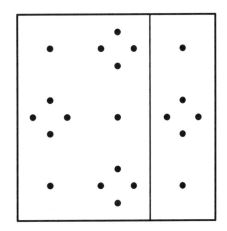

264

A HARD DIVISION

A woman had a piece of chocolate as shown (the bottom is twice as long as the flat top or perpendicular right side). She wanted to give each of her four daughters a reward for their good school work but was unsure how to cut the chocolate evenly. One of her daughters immediately devised a scheme that divided it into four equal pieces of the same shape as the original. How did she do it?

265

DIVIDING THE HEXAGON

Draw a hexagon and then see if you can divide it into 12 equal and identical four-sided figures.

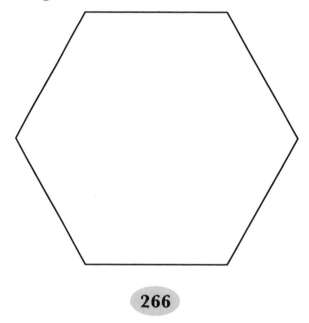

266

FOUR-SIDED DIFFICULTIES

How many different squares and rectangles can you outline in this figure?

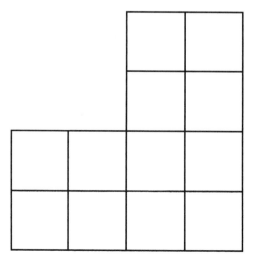

267

SHARE AND SHARE ALIKE

Four friends chipped in and bought a 100 x 100 foot vacant lot near the beach with plans to build four small souvenir shops on it. Since a local law stated that individual buildings on the same lot had to be at least ten feet from each other, what were the largest buildings of equal size that the four of them could build?

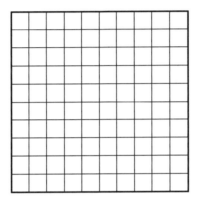

268

THE PLUS SIGN

Draw 25 dots to form a square. Then see if you can connect 12 of the dots with straight lines so as to form a plus sign. The plus sign will have five dots inside it and eight dots outside it.

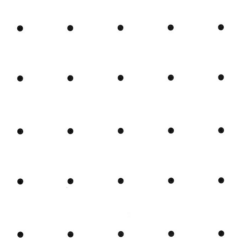

269

POINT TO POINT

Draw 13 dots as shown on the left. Then see if you can connect them as shown on the right by drawing one continuous line that doesn't retrace any line. You're allowed to visit the same dot more than once.

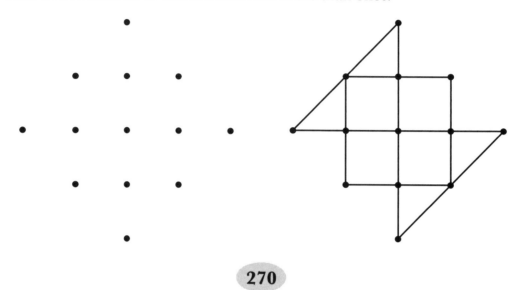

270

ROCKET SHIP OF TRIANGLES

Twelve triangles have been stacked up in the shape of a rocket ship. Can you divide the rocket into four equal-sized pieces, each of the same shape?

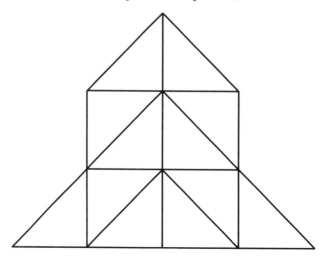

271

THE APPLE GROVE

One day a gentleman farmer decided he would plant a small grove of apple trees on his property.

"Here, Caleb," he said to his worker, "plant these nine trees in eight rows, with three trees in each row."

It took the worker some time to figure it out, but he was successful in the end. Can you draw the arrangement?

272

THREE LETTERS

Draw a square that's divided into 25 smaller squares, blackening four of them as shown. The puzzle is to find three letters that can be used to fill the 21 white squares, one letter per square, so that the same five-letter word is spelled in 12 different directions.

You might discover more than one trio of letters that work. We've listed 17 possibilities in the answer section (no proper names). How many of them can you find?

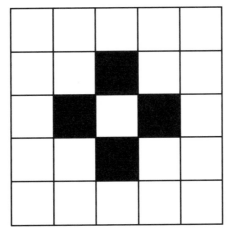

End of PENCIL and PAPER Puzzles

Answers to these puzzles start on page 204

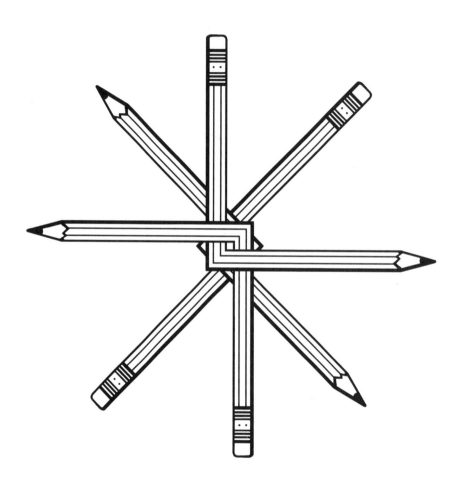

Teaser
PUZZLES

273

WHAT A BIRD

A woman read about a bird that could outrun a horse and roar like a lion, but couldn't fly. Was this bird fictional or real? *Ostrich*

274

LITTLE BODY PARTS

There are ten parts of the human body spelled with just three letters, yet few people can come up with more than seven. How many can you name?

bum Tum eye ear
leg
Toe arm

275

FINGERS AND THUMBS

What number would you end up with if you multiplied the number of thumbs a person has by the number of fingers? *20*

276

ANIMALS AT THE CIRCUS

A group of animals decided to go the circus one day, but they had to have money to get in. The duck got in all right. Why? Because he had a bill. The frog got in: He had a green back. The deer got in because he had the doe. The doe got in because she had a buck. The hog got in because he had four quarters. But the skunk did not get in. To be sure, he had a (s)cent, but why was he not admitted?

277

THE CLOCK STRIKES

If it takes a clock 30 seconds to strike six o'clock, how long will it take it to strike twelve o'clock?

278

AUGUST

August was a hound pup who was always barking, jumping, and biting. One day he barked and jumped at a very ornery mule and then bit its hindquarters. Appropriately, the next day was the first of September. Why was that appropriate?

279

THE SECOND DAY

Ask someone if they will pronounce several words, and bet them that they will not be able to do so correctly. First have them pronounce t-o, next t-o-o, and finally t-w-o. Then say, "How do you pronounce the second day of the week?" Most people will pronounce it incorrectly. Can you guess why?

280

WHAT'S IN A NAME?

A father bought a ranch and presented it to his two sons. They planned to raise cattle on it for the market. After considerable deliberation, the two boys decided to call the ranch "Focus." Why on earth was that an appropriate name?

281

THE RIDDLE OF EUROPE

There are five European countries, one of which is also partially in Asia, that end in "y." Can you name them all in 20 seconds? Each is well known, but it's pretty hard to think of them in a hurry.

282

WAKE UP AND GIVE

This is one of those that seem obvious, like "Who was it that wrote Tchaikovsky's Sixth Symphony?" The question is: How long will an eight-day alarm clock run without winding?

283

BROTHERS AND SISTERS

Mr. and Mrs. Hoffman have six daughters. Each of the daughters has a brother. How many persons are there in the Hoffman family? 14

284

DOT, DOT, DOT

Can you think of the one word in the English language and the name of one country, each of which is spelled with three dotted letters in a row?

285

NINE IN ONE

What seven-letter word, without rearranging any of its letters, contains nine shorter words reading from left to right?

286

EYESIGHT TEST

Can the average person see things farther away in the daytime or at night?

287

Night?

HOLE NUMBERS

A professor asked one of his students how much dirt there was in a rectangular hole that measured 2 x 3 x 4 feet. The student said 24 cubic feet. Was he right?

288

THE JACKS

Two of the jacks in an ordinary pack of cards are drawn so that one eye is visible. The other two are drawn with two eyes visible on each. Given that, what is the total number of eyes showing on all four jacks?

289

STRIKE TWO

See if you can remove two letters from each of these words so that the remaining letters, still in the same order, spell out a synonym of the original word: EVACUATE and MATCHES.

290

THE 17 EGGS

Mathematical sharks can tell in ten seconds or less how much 17 eggs would cost if sold at 12 cents a dozen. Can you?

291

THE FLAG RAISING

In the town of Smithville, the flag pole is 105 feet high. On Memorial Day, a flag that measures five feet from top to bottom is raised. If the top of the flag is five feet above the ground when it starts, how many feet does the top of the flag travel before reaching its final position on the pole?

292

THE PEACOCK'S EGG

A wealthy Englishman, Lord Gotrocks, was very fond of the peacocks he kept on his grounds. One day, however, one of his most beautiful birds wandered over to a neighboring estate owned by Lord Duffer. While the peacock was there, it laid an egg, which Lord Duffer immediately took as his own. Lord Gotrocks objected. Who owned the egg?

293

THE EXPERIMENT

A scientist was conducting a series of experiments and noticed that a certain chemical reaction took 80 minutes when he was wearing his lab coat. When he didn't wear his lab coat, however, the same reaction always took an hour and 20 minutes. Why do you think this was?

294

THE SILENT PARROT

One day, a woman bought a parrot that the pet store owner promised would be able to repeat every word it heard. Over the next few months, however, the woman was very disappointed that the bird didn't repeat a single word. Nevertheless, the store owner was truthful. How could this be?

295

ONE WAY OR THE OTHER

What word, when spelled forward, can mean a hint or an extremity and when spelled backward can mean a hole or a racecar area?

296

WHAT TIME WAS IT?

A man had a clock in his front hallway that struck every half hour. On the full hours, it sounded a number of chimes equal to the hour. On the half hours, it struck just once. Arriving home late one night, he heard the clock chime once as he opened the front door. A half hour later, it again chimed once. For the next two half-hour intervals, it also chimed just once each. What time was it when the man came in?

End of TEASER Puzzles

Answers to these puzzles start on page 209

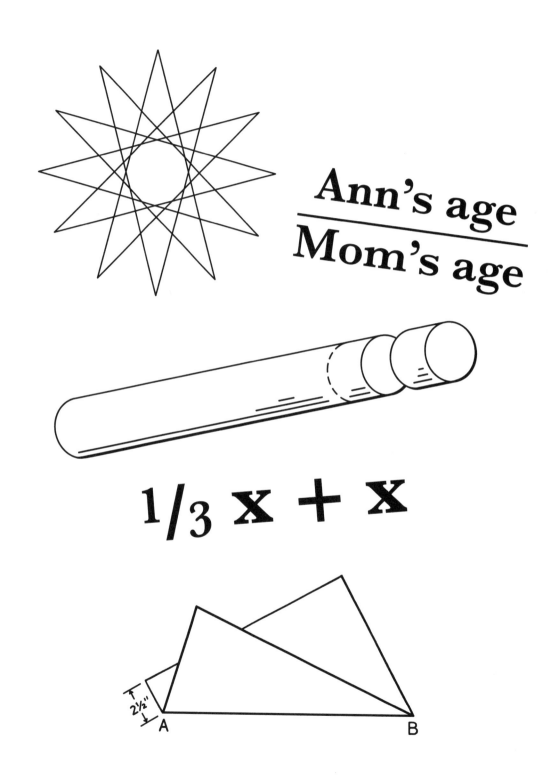

$$\frac{\text{Ann's age}}{\text{Mom's age}}$$

$$\frac{1}{3}\,x + x$$

Mathematical PUZZLES

297

THE NON-SHRINKING WINDOW

Mrs. Smithers had a house in which one of the windows was a square measuring two feet wide by two feet high. After boarding up half of the window, it was still a square and it still measured two feet across and two feet from top to bottom. How was this was possible?

298

THE FIVE PIECES OF CHAIN

A man had five pieces of chain, each made up of three links. He wanted to join the five pieces together to make one big chain of fifteen links and went to a blacksmith to see how much it would cost.

"Well," said the blacksmith, "I will charge you 50 cents for cutting a link and $1.00 for welding a link. Any bending that's required is free."

Given those prices, what is the smallest amount of money for which the job could be done?

299

CUTTING THE POLE

You have a ten-foot pole that needs to be cut it into ten equal pieces. If it takes ten seconds to make each cut, how long will the job take?

300

AUTOMOBILE RIDE

In the morning, a man drives from home to work at an average speed of 20 miles per hour. At the end of the day, he drives back home over the same road at any average speed of 30 miles per hour. What is his average speed for the round trip?

301

BALL AND BAT

A boy bought a baseball and a bat, paying $1.25 for both items. If the ball cost 25 cents more than the bat, how much did each cost?

302

FOUR GALLONS

You need to measure out four gallons of water, but all you have is a five-gallon can and a three-gallon can. How can you accomplish the task?

303

THE SNAIL IN THE WELL

A snail starts at the bottom of a 16-foot well and crawls up four feet each day. Each night, however, the poor thing slips back three feet. On what day will the snail reach the top of the well?

304

THE TWO TRAINS

Here is a famous old puzzle that continues to perplex solvers:

One train leaves New York for Washington and travels at a speed of 25 miles per hour. At the same time, another train leaves Washington for New York and speeds along on a parallel track at 50 miles per hour. When the two trains meet, which is nearer New York?

305

HOW MANY COOKIES?

A mother is dividing up some cookies among her three sons. To the oldest, she gives half of the cookies plus half a cookie. To her middle son, she gives half of what she has left plus half a cookie. Finally, she gives her youngest son half of what she now has left plus half a cookie, which leaves her with no cookies. At no time is a cookie cut, broken, or divided. How many does she begin with?

306

HOW MANY DINNERS?

There were seven friends who decided that they would all dine together every evening provided they could sit in a different arrangement each time. They would use the same table, always with seven chairs in the same spots. How many dinners could the seven of them eat before exhausting all possible arrangements?

307

THE TWO BOOKS

A two-volume set of books sits on a bookshelf with the spines facing out, volume I to the left of volume II. Each book is three inches thick and each cover is 1/4-inch thick. If a bookworm starts on the title page of volume I and eats through to the last page of volume II, how far did it travel?

308

THE SUITCASE OF CASH

Five members of a bank-robbing gang came to a hotel one night, each taking a separate room. The gang's leader had with him a large suitcase containing money from that day's heist, which was to be evenly divided between the five of them in the morning. Since the gang members didn't trust him alone with the suitcase, it was agreed that the unsuspecting clerk would safeguard it for the night.

Soon after they'd retired for the night, one member of the gang went downstairs and asked for the suitcase. Once in the parlor, he proceeded to divide up the money. When he'd finished, there were five equal stacks of money sitting on the table with one dollar left over. He tucked one of the stacks into his nightshirt, tossed the other four back in the suitcase, and gave the clerk the extra dollar for his troubles. He then returned to his room.

Throughout the night, while the leader slept, the other three members of the gang snuck downstairs and did likewise. Each counted up the remaining money, which always made five equal stacks with one dollar left over. One stack was taken and the clerk was given a dollar upon returning the suitcase.

In the morning, the five of them assembled as planned and divided up what was left in the suitcase. Again, the amount divided evenly into five portions with one dollar left over for the clerk. What is the smallest number of dollars that the suitcase could have contained to begin with?

309

THE HERD OF CATTLE

A farmer once died and left a herd of cattle to his five sons. The first son was to get $1/3$ of the herd, the second $1/4$ of the herd, the third $1/6$ of the herd, the fourth $1/8$ of the herd, and the fifth $1/9$ of the herd. Unfortunately, the sons found that the herd could not be divided evenly in this way.

Just as they were puzzling over the situation, a neighbor came along and figured out that by lending them two of his cows, everything would divide evenly. Each son received his proper share of the herd, after which the neighbor took back his two cows.

How many cows were there in the herd and how many did each son get?

310

THE BAND OF STEEL

An engineer is said to have originated this problem. Assume that the equator is an even 25,000 miles in circumference and that a band of steel is fitted tightly around it. If an additional 12 inches is added to the band, approximately how far off the earth will the band be?

311

THREE MAKES 12

Draw the figure shown below on a piece of paper and then see if you can put the digits 1–7 in the seven circles so that the three digits in every straight line add up to 12.

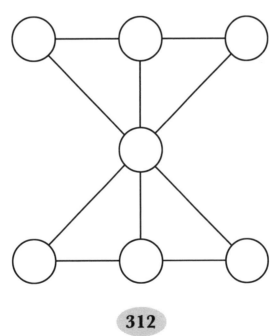

312

A HORSE DEAL

A man had two horses. He sold one of them on Tuesday for $198 and made a profit of ten percent. On Wednesday, he sold the other one for $198 and took a loss of ten percent. Tallying up his two deals on Thursday, did he show a net profit or a loss?

313

THREE MAKES 18

Draw a diagram like the one below on a piece of paper. Then see if you can place the numbers 1–11 in the eleven circles so that the three numbers in every straight line add up to 18.

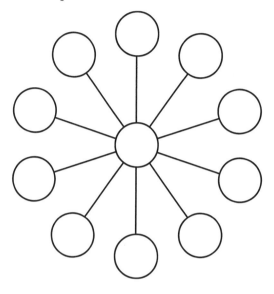

314

SIXTY MILES PER HOUR

One day, a motorist came to a hill that was a ten-mile drive up one side and a ten-mile drive down the other. He drove up the hill at an average speed of 30 miles per hour. How fast will he have to drive down the other side to average 60 miles per hour for the entire 20-mile distance?

315

STRIPS OF PAPER

Imagine three sheets of paper, each measuring 20 inches by 40 inches. These are to be cut into strips two inches wide by 20 inches long. If it takes three seconds to cut each strip, what is the shortest possible time in which the cutting can be completed? Folding of the sheets is not allowed.

316

HOW MANY TRAINS?

A woman leaves Westville by train at 9:00 P.M. and will arrive in Eastville at 9:00 P.M. the next night. Trains traveling in the reverse direction leave every hour on the hour on a set of parallel tracks. From the moment her train departs Westville until the time it pulls into Eastville, how many different trains bound for Westville will she see? Trains travel at the same speed in both directions, and we're assuming the woman is looking out a window that faces the other track.

317

HOW OLD IS ANN?

Ann is 1/5 as old as her mother. Her mother's age, when lessened by one, can be divided evenly by two, three, four, six, and eight. Her mother's age, when not lessened by one, can be divided evenly by five. How old is Ann?

318

FORTY POUNDS

You have an iron bar that weighs 40 pounds. See if you can figure out how to cut it into four pieces so that those pieces can then be used on a balance-scale to weigh objects from 1–40 pounds (full pounds only). Remember that a balance-scale allows you to put one or more weights on each side in addition to the object being weighed.

319

GIVE AND TAKE

Jim gave Jack as many dollars as Jack already had. When Jack received this money, he asked Jim how much he had left. Upon being told, he immediately gave this amount back to Jim. Jim, who was equally generous, gave Jack back as many dollars as Jack had left. This left Jim without any money and gave Jack $80 altogether. How much did each one have to begin with?

320

HOT AND COLD WATER

A bathtub can be filled using the cold water tap in six minutes and 40 seconds. The hot water tap will fill the tub in eight minutes exactly. When the tub is full and the stopper is removed, the water will run out in 13 minutes and 20 seconds (the drain is hopelessly clogged).

If the stopper is removed and water is coming into the tub from both faucets, how long will it take the tub to fill?

321

NICE IF YOU CAN GET IT

A store owner badly needed a worker but couldn't afford to pay much. After putting a sign in the window, a fellow strolled in, discovered the man's predicament, and suggested a temporary arrangement. He said he'd work every day for a month and would take only one penny for his first day's work. His pay would then double on each successive day, two cents for the second day, four cents for the third day, eight cents for the fourth day, and so on. The store owner jumped at the offer and hired him on the spot.

Did he get his wish for a cheap employee or not?

322

A BIG DEAL IN FARMLAND

While in town one day, a farmer was asked by one of the local smart alecks if he had any land to sell. The farmer thought about this for a moment and then replied, "Well, I do have a good piece of bottom land I'm not using. I could sell it to you real cheap."

"Great," the smart aleck said. "How big is it?"

"It's a triangle," said the farmer. "It's longest side is six miles and each of the other two sides is three miles long. I don't know the exact acreage, but it's yours for $100."

"I'll take it!" the smart aleck immediately replied, paying him $100 on the spot.

Can you figure out who got the better end of the deal?

323

DOLLARS AND CENTS

A man went into a store with a wad of one-dollar bills and nearly as many pennies. When he left, he'd spent exactly half of his money. Counting his change, he noted the following facts:

1. The number of pennies he had left was equal to the number of one-dollar bills he had before he entered the store.
2. The number of pennies he started with was twice the number of one-dollar bills he had after he left the store.

How much money did he start with and how much did he spend?

324

AIRPLANE RACE

Two planes take off at the same time from the same point to race to a point and back. Plane A travels at 180 miles per hour on the way out and 240 miles per hour on the return trip. Plane B covers the entire distance at an average speed of 210 miles per hour. Which plane wins the race, or is it a tie?

325

THE ENTHUSIASTIC BEE

A bee alighted on the head of a horse rider whose horse was trotting eastbound at a steady five miles per hour. Some distance ahead on the same path, another horse and rider were approaching westbound, also at five miles per hour.

When the two horses were 20 miles apart, the bee left his perch on the first steed and flew toward the second horse at a rate of ten miles per hour. Upon reaching the second horse, the insect immediately turned around and sped back at the same rate to the first horse.

If the bee kept up this rather inane performance until the two riders met, how far did he travel from the moment he left the first horse?

326

THE GUALALA WATER BOTTLE

In the Gualala Desert, water is scarce and is sold by the bottle. But bottles are even scarcer than water. A visitor who recently returned from the area reported that he paid $1.05 for a bottle filled with water, and the bottle cost $1.00 more than its contents. How much did the water cost?

327

HOW OLD WAS I?

The year in which my grandfather was born, a perfect square, when subtracted from the year in which my daughter was born, another perfect square, gives my grandfather's age when he died. If my grandfather had lived, I would have been exactly half his age in 1943. How old was I in 1943?

328

HOW LONG IS THE FOLD?

A standard piece of paper measuring 8 1/2 x 11 inches is folded as shown below. Can you figure out the length of the fold AB to the nearest 1/4 inch?

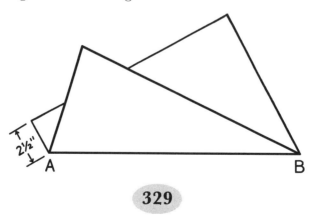

329

THE HUNGRY CATS

If three cats can eat three bowls of food in three minutes, how long will it take 100 cats to eat 100 bowls of food?

330

WEIGH THIS FISH

What is the weight of a fish if it weighs ten pounds plus half its weight?

331

THE TWELVE-POINTED STAR

Place the even numbers 2–22, one next to each point on the star, so that the sum of any two adjacent numbers equals the sum of the two numbers directly opposite on the star. The top point has two numbers on it, either of which may be paired with an adjacent number. Every other point will have just one number.

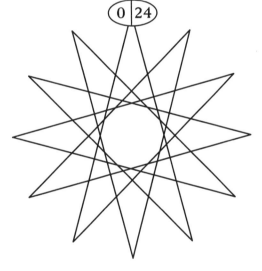

332

HARE AND HOUND

A hound chases a hare, taking two 10-foot bounds every second. The hare takes three 6-foot bounds every second. At this rate, the hound will catch the hare in one minute, but just ten seconds before that occurs, the hare scoots in his hole. What was the distance between the hare and the hound at the start of the chase, and how much of that distance had the hound made up when the hare disappeared in his hole?

333

THE PEANUT-EATING MONKEYS

Four monkeys can eat four sacks of peanuts in three minutes. How many monkeys will it take to eat 100 sacks of peanuts in one hour?

334

HOW MANY STEPS?

A girl starts from a given point. If, each time that she takes two steps forward, she must take one backward, how many steps will she have to take to reach a point five steps ahead of her starting point?

335

THE THIRTY CENTS PUZZLE

Without using pennies, see if you can figure out how many different combinations of coins will make 30 cents.

336

WHAT DID THE SUIT COST?

A man once bought a fine suit for which he paid $30.00 more than $1/4$ of its price. How much did he pay for the suit?

337

JANE AND JOHN

The sum of Jane's and John's ages is 22. However, Jane will be seven times as old as John is now when she becomes twice his age. How old is Jane?

338

GROWING PAINS

A father is five times as old as his son. In fifteen years he will be only twice as old. How old is the father at present?

339

FILL UP THE TANK

It takes 30 minutes to completely fill a tank. If, however, a hole allows 1/3 of the water that is entering the tank to escape, how long will it then take to fill the tank?

340

LAWN MOWING

If it takes a man two hours to mow a square lawn, each side of which is 100 feet long, how long will it take him to mow a square lawn whose sides are 50 feet long? We're assuming that he mows each lawn at the same rate.

341

HOW MANY MEN?

A landscaping job takes a certain number of men as many days to complete as there are men working. If the addition of six men would complete the job in just one day, how many men were working?

342

THE BANK TELLER'S MISTAKE

In cashing a check, a bank teller mistakenly paid out in dollars what should have been paid out in cents, and vice versa. After the recipient of the incorrect sum had spent 62 cents, there remained twice the amount that had been written on the check. What was the amount written on the check?

343

THE FRIENDLY PROFESSOR

A kindhearted professor once shook hands with each of his six students while thanking them for their good work during the term. Following suit, the students then all shook hands with one another. How many handshakes were there all together?

344

SHE WAS THE MARRYING KIND

A wealthy woman, who was divorced eight times over, decided to give a dinner party for her eight ex-husbands, each of which had been divorced numerous times. If each ex-husband wanted to attend with one of his ex-wives, what is the minimum number of people the hostess would have at her dinner party?

345

HOW OLD IS ANN?...AGAIN

Here's another variation on the "How Old is Ann?" puzzle, and it's no cinch to solve. The story is short and sweet and goes as follows:

If Mary is twice as old as Ann was when Mary was as old as Ann is now, and Mary is 32, how old is Ann?

346

THE BILL

Mr. Rice had breakfast one day at a diner with Mr. Stutts. When it came time to pay the check, it was found that Mr. Rice had as many one-dollar bills as Mr. Stutts had quarters. Rather than each man paying separately, Mr. Rice paid his share of the bill, $6, to Mr. Stutts. At that point, Mr. Stutts had four times as much money as Mr. Rice. How much money did each have at the beginning?

347

PLAIN LIVING

Mr. Asterbilt went to the Ritz one day for lunch. Looking over the menu, he noticed that there were 11 appetizers, 26 entrees, and 12 kinds of desserts. In addition, there were 13 wine selections offered. How many different meal combinations was Mr. Asterbilt facing if each combination consisted of one item from each of the four categories?

348

THE COUNTERFEIT PENNY

A pile of 32 pennies contains one counterfeit. It looks exactly the same but weighs less. What is the minimum number of times the pennies must be weighed using a scale-balance to know for certain which is the countefeit?

349

FASHION PARADE

A woman counted the items in her wardrobe one day and found that she had seven hats and five dresses. How many ways could she combine these without wearing the same two twice?

350

A PROBLEM IN SUBTRACTION

What one digit, when put in each of the four blanks, makes this subtraction problem true.

$$
\begin{array}{r}
\_\,\_\,1 \\
-\ \ \_\,0\,\_ \\
\hline
1\,9
\end{array}
$$

351

RAILROAD PROBLEM

A railroad line has 15 stations that are spread out in a straight east-west line. How many different trips are possible, starting at one station and ending at any other station? Each trip must go entirely in one direction, east or west.

352

THE HUNDRED YEARS PUZZLE

Mrs. Green and Mrs. Brown's ages, when added together, total 121 years. If Mrs. Green's age, when multiplied by four and divided by seven, gives Mrs. Brown's age, how old is each?

353

THE DRAWBRIDGE

The two halves of a drawbridge are each 40 feet long. If the length of each half is increased by ten feet, how far above their usual fully lowered position will the two halves meet?

354

THE "TWICE AS MUCH" WILL

Mr. Bogsworth once left a will which read:

To Bob, twice as much as to Betty.
To Brian, twice as much as to Bob.
To Bill, twice as much as to Brian.

If his estate was valued at $45,000, how much did each of the four heirs receive?

355

THE TWO AUTOMOBILES

One automobile traveled at 48 miles per hour and another at 60 miles per hour. How much of a head start did the slower one need for the two automobiles to complete the same 720-mile trip at the same time?

356

SOUR APPLES

A small boy once snuck into an orchard and took some apples. On the way out, he ran into the farmer and his two sons. Frightened to death, he gave the farmer half his take. He then gave one son half of the remaining apples and the other son half of the apples left after that. For good measure, he gave all three of them one more apple each. This left him with two apples, which the farmer let him keep. Given all that, how many apples did he start with?

357

THE HIKERS

Two hikers set out together on a long trek. One walked 1/4 of a mile per hour faster than the other and finished half an hour earlier. If both walked 34 miles, at what rate did each walk?

358

HE DID PRETTY WELL

A man, who had been married for three years, spent 2/5 of his yearly income on his family, 1/4 on entertaining business associates, and 1/10 on travel. If he saved $45,000 during those three years, what was his annual income?

359

TIRED AND RETIRED

An automobile dealer ordered 1,000 tires, which was enough to furnish a spare tire for all the wheels of all the automobiles and motorcycles he had on hand. If altogether he had 296 vehicles, how many autos and how many motorcycles did he have?

360

CAPITAL GAINS

A man starts with $10,000 and increases his wealth by 50 percent every three years. How much will he have in 12 years?

361

COUNTING SHEEP

Bill Bardham had 170 sheep in his flock. His neighbor, Will Worthman, had 30. They bought an equal number of sheep at the annual livestock auction. After doing so, Bill owned three times as many sheep as Will. How many did they each buy?

362

STEAMBOAT TRIP

A steamboat travels downstream at 15 miles per hour and upstream at ten miles per hour. If the upstream leg of the boat's daily roundtrip takes four hours more than the downstream leg, how long is its route?

363

BROTHERS AND SISTERS

A boy and his sister were walking down the street one afternoon when they met the proverbial kindly old man. When the old man asked the youngsters about the size of their family, the boy quickly piped up.

"I have as many brothers as I have sisters," he proudly stated.

Not to be left out, the girl added, "I have three times as many brothers as I have sisters."

Can you tell how many boys and girls there were in their family?

364

1, 2, 3, 4, 5, 6, 7, 8, 9

What is the smallest number divisible by all of the numbers 1–9?

365

A LITTER OF PIGS

A farmer was asked how many pigs he had. "Well," he said, "if I had just as many more again, plus half as many more, plus another $1\frac{1}{2}$ times more, I would have three dozen." How many pigs did he have?

366

THE CURIOUS CLOCK

Old Mr. Glover has a clock that for some reason stops for a minute every ten minutes. What is the shortest amount of time it takes for the minute hand to completely circle the clock face?

367

HOW MANY DUCKS?

A farmer was asked how many ducks he had. "Well," he said, "they ran down the path just now, and I saw one duck in front of two ducks, a duck behind two ducks, and a duck between two ducks." What is the fewest number of ducks he had?

368

THREESCORE AND...?

A young girl was doing a school biography about her grandfather, who was quite the math whiz. When she asked him for a summary of his life, he gave the following response:

> After being born, I spent the first $1/4$ of my life in California. For the next $1/6$ of my life, I lived in Pittsburgh working as an accountant. Immediately after that, I moved to New Jersey, where I was a math teacher for the next $1/3$ of my life, followed by 12 years in upstate New York where I was a college professor. I then retired and moved to Florida where I've now lived for the latest $1/12$ of my life to date.

How old do you suppose the spritely number cruncher was?

End of MATHEMATICAL Puzzles

Answers to these puzzles start on page 211

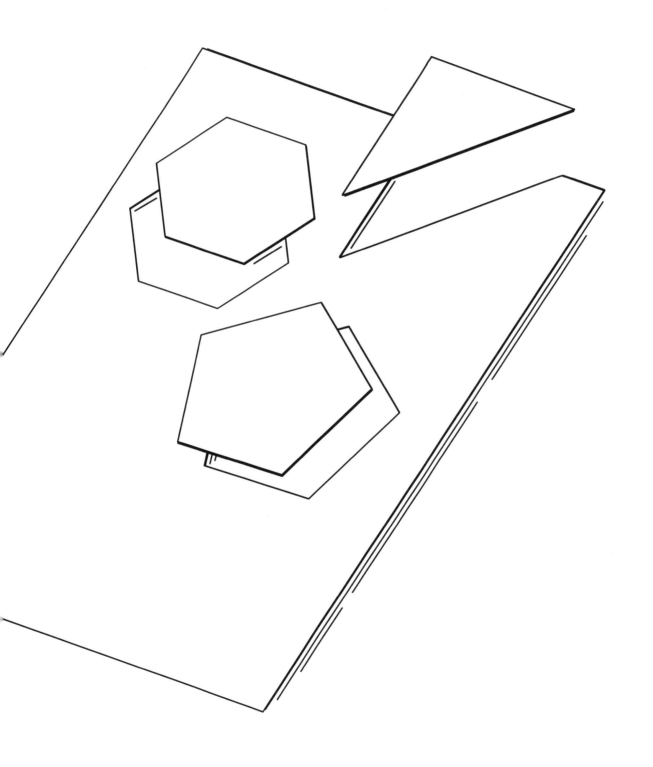

Cut-Out

PUZZLES

369

THE NINE-PIECE SQUARE

Cut out a square from a piece of heavy paper or thin cardboard and draw pencil lines on it as shown. Cut along the lines with a pair of scissors, mix the pieces up, then see if you or a friend can put the square back together again.

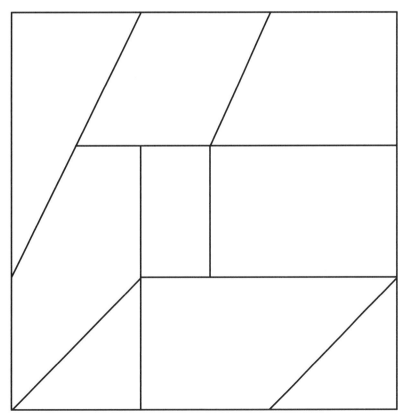

370

THE OCTAGON

Trace the three shapes on the left and cut out four of each. Then see if you can fit the 12 pieces together to make an octagon of the size shown at right.

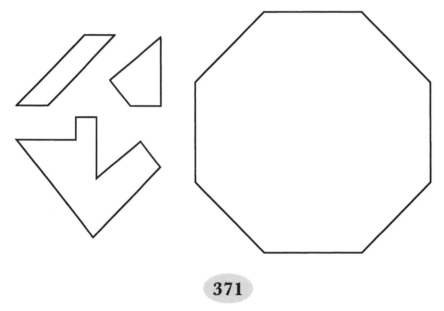

371

THE H PUZZLE

Draw a letter H and add pencil lines as shown. Cut along the lines to form seven pieces, then see if you can put it back together.

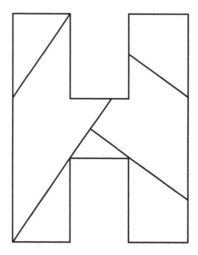

372

THE SIX-PIECE SQUARE

Here is another cut-up square, this time divided into six pieces. Cut it apart and see if you can reassemble it.

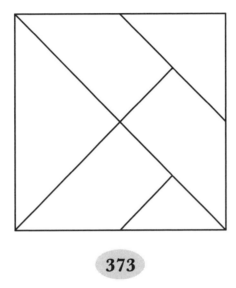

373

THE COMPLICATED SQUARE

Trace the three shapes below and cut out four of each. Then see if you can fit the 12 pieces together to form a square.

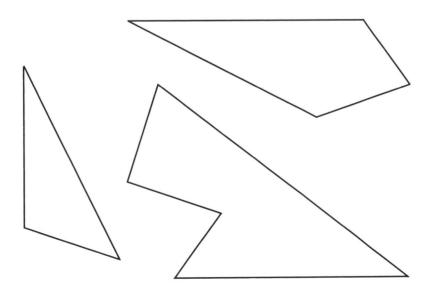

374

THE T PUZZLE

Draw a T and then cut it into four pieces as shown. Putting it back together isn't as simple as it might seem.

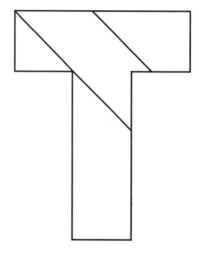

375

THE FIVE-PIECE CROSS

Trace the two shapes shown below. Cut out four of the "Z" shapes and one rectangle. The puzzle is to fit the five pieces together to form a cross (a plus sign with a longer bottom arm).

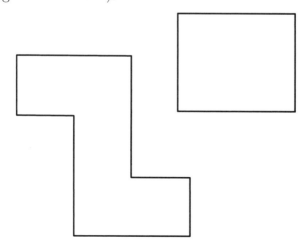

376

THE HOUSE AND PORCH

Cut out a "house and porch" shape to the dimensions shown. Now see if you can make two straight cuts, resulting in three pieces that will fit together to form a square.

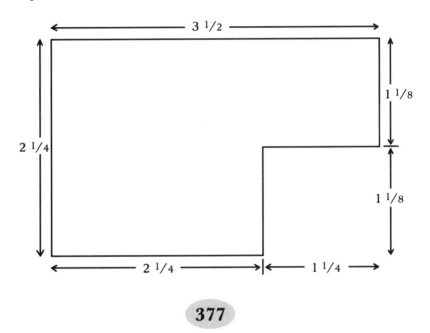

377

ANOTHER CUT-UP SQUARE

Cut up a square as shown, then see if you can put it back together.

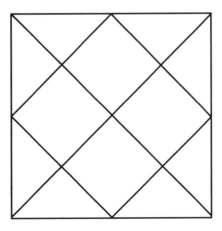

378

THE ROMAN CROSS

Cut up a cross into five pieces as shown. It is fairly difficult to fit these pieces together again if you don't know the solution.

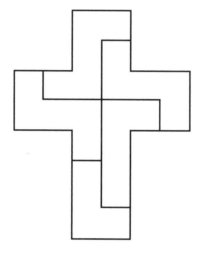

379

PLUS TO SQUARE

Here's a difficult challenge. Cut out a plus sign so that all 12 sides are equal and all angles are 90 degrees. Now see if you can cut it into four pieces that can be fit together to form a square.

380

SQUARE TO OBLONG

Here's another one that'll test you. Cut out a piece of paper $2^1/_2$ inches square. Now see if you can cut it into two pieces that can be put together to form a rectangle that is 2 x $3^1/_8$ inches.

381

THE FIVE-PIECE SQUARE

Cut up a square as shown, then see if you can put it back together.

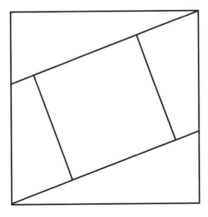

382

FIVE MAKE A CROSS

This puzzle, which has been handed down from generation to generation, is just as tricky today as it was centuries ago. Trace and cut out three of the triangles. Trace the other two pieces and cut out one of each. The puzzle is to fit the five pieces together to form a cross.

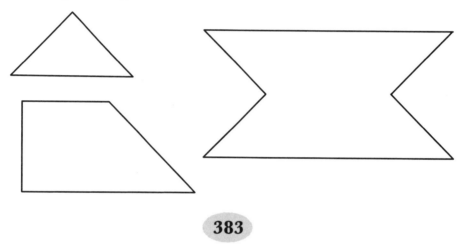

383

THE DIAMOND AND SQUARE

The four irregularly shaped pieces shown below can be put together to form both a diamond and a square. Trace the shapes and cut them out, then see how clever an assembler you are.

384

TANGRAMS

This is probably the greatest of all cut-out-and-put-together puzzles, and is one that can provide endless hours of amusement. The seven tangram pieces, known in China as long ago as 3,000 B.C., were originally cut from leaves, and later fashioned out of parchment. The puzzle has intrigued countless numbers over the centuries, including Napoleon, who used it to ease his boredom during his exile on St. Helena.

The tangram pieces are made by cutting a square as shown. All seven of the pieces must then be put together to form different figures, usually caricatures of people or animals. Make your own tangram pieces using heavy paper or thin cardboard.

Two tangram figures are shown on the right for you to try, a woman carrying a parcel and a jumping dog, but there are scores of others you can create yourself.

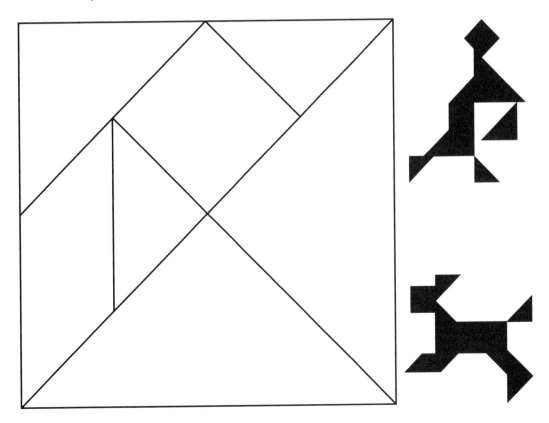

385

TORMENTORS

This is a puzzle that uses the same principle as tangrams. The difference is that a set of eight shapes are used to form geometric figures. Hundreds of different figures can be made with the tormentors' pieces, a few of which are shown here. First, see if you can recreate these three (the solutions are in the answer section), then make your own. All eight pieces need to be used to create each figure.

386

THE HEXAGON

Trace the five irregular shapes shown below and cut them out. Then see if you can fit them together to form a hexagon with six equal sides.

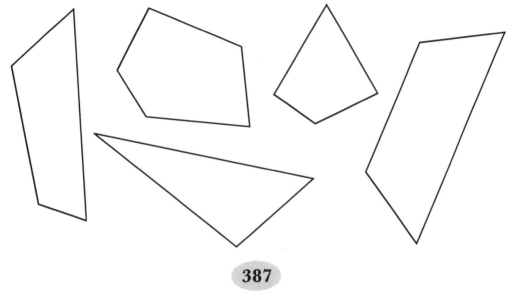

387

CROSS-CUT

Draw a grid of guidelines $1/2$ inch apart, then outline a notched shape as shown and cut it out. The puzzle is to make two straight cuts, resulting in four pieces that will fit together to form a square.

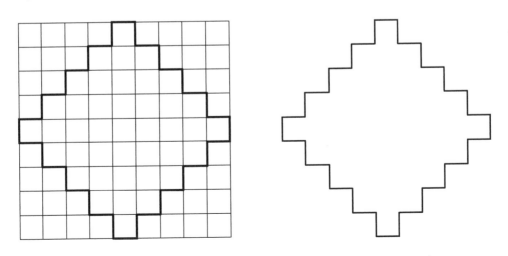

388

THE FOUR-PIECE SQUARE

Trace the four pieces shown and cut them out. Then see if you can arrange them to form a square.

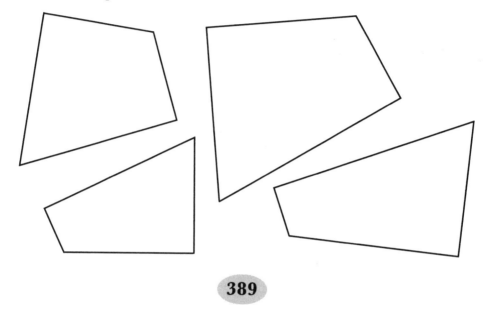

389

TRIANGLES AND SQUARE

Trace the pieces below, then cut out four of the triangles and one square. The puzzle is to put the five pieces together to form a square.

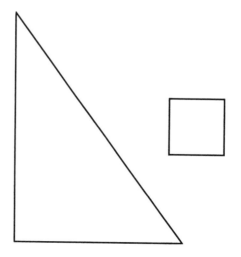

390

CUT-OUT STAR

Another unusual figure to put together is a star. The pieces shown here, when properly assembled, form a perfect five-pointed star.

391

CUT-OUT LETTERS

You can make excellent cut-out puzzles with any letter of the alphabet. Draw outlines of letters that spell yours or a friend's name, cut them up, and you've got an instant handmade puzzle.

End of CUT-OUT Puzzles

Answers to these puzzles start on page 219

Bonus PUZZLES

392

CHECKERBOARD PUZZLE

Get out your checkerboard and put eight checkers on it. Then see if you can put the checkers on the squares so that no two checkers are on the same vertical, horizontal, or diagonal line. There are a number of possible solutions, but it is usually fairly hard to discover even one of them.

393

THE HANDCUFFS PUZZLE

This is a classic puzzle for two people. Tie two string handcuffs around yours and a friend's wrists, making sure they're linked as shown. The puzzle is to unlink the strings without slipping your hands out of the wrist loops or untying, cutting, or damaging the strings in any way.

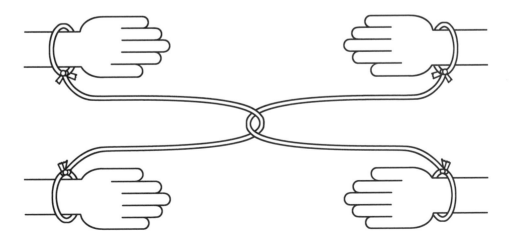

394

THE THREE DICE

Given that the number of pips on opposite sides of a die always add up to seven, what are the pip counts on the four faces that are touching each other? The pip design (their positions on the faces in relation to each other) is consistent for all the dice.

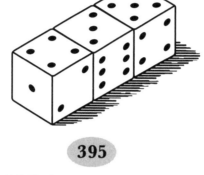

395

DICE SKYSCRAPERS

Which skyscraper's six bottom faces add up to a greater sum? Opposite sides always add up to seven and the pip design is consistent from die to die.

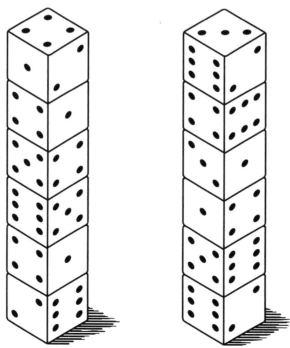

396

A PLAYING CARD PUZZLE

Take all four of each of the face cards and aces from a pack of cards. Then see if you can arrange the 16 of them in four rows of four each so that there is only one of each suit and denomination in each horizontal row, in each vertical column, and along both diagonals.

397

THE 10-CARD SQUARE

Take ten cards from a pack of cards, ace through ten. Then see if you can arrange them as shown so that the numbers of the cards on each side add up to 18 (aces equal one). Four cards are added together in the top and bottom rows; three cards are added together in the two sides columns.

398

PLAY TIME PUZZLE CARDS

This is a different kind of a puzzle for one player or a group. Divide a piece of heavy paper or thin cardboard into eight equal parts and then print the word "PLAYTIME" on it as shown. Cut out the eight cards along the lines, then use them to answer the clues on these two pages.

A time limit of 15 or 20 seconds can be imposed for coming up with each answer if you like.

A. Pick and arrange cards to spell the five-letter words that fit these clues:

    1. a kind of tree
    2. enough
    3. without any contents
    4. a Southern European country
    5. subtly suggest
    6. pants crease
    7. coin material
    8. _____-mouthed (wishy-washy)
    9. a flower part
    10. having a lot of substance
    11. hair braid
    12. a dish

B. Spell these common first names for people:

    1. four three-letter names (twelve are listed in the answers)
    2. two common names that together use all eight cards

C. Spell the four-letter words that fit these clues:

    1. send out
    2. small news note
    3. device that gives light
    4. brewery grain
    5. that which is sent by post
    6. companion
    7. horse-race distance
    8. part of the hand
    9. top of the head
    10. sound, as bells
    11. trapper's prize
    12. a feeling of compassion
    13. request for aid
    14. story
    15. race's finish line
    16. sports group
    17. hobbling
    18. it's set by a printer
    19. an Ivy League university
    20. puppy's cry
    21. heap
    22. ashen
    23. thaw
    24. a green fruit

D. And finally, spell the six-letter words that fit these clues:

    1. punctual
    2. pierce with a point

399

THE BOOT PUZZLE

This little known but very good puzzle may be made using heavy paper or thin cardboard (the dimensions below are for an 8 1/2 x 11 inch sheet).

Once you've put the puzzle together, anyone who doesn't know how it was made will find it extremely difficult to remove the boots.

Step 1: Fold your sheet of paper in half and cut out the three shapes.
Step 2: Unfold A and slip it over the lower prong of B (which is still folded).
Step 3: Hang C over one half of B's lower prong.
Step 4: Slide A on top of C.
Step 5: Unfold B and you've made your puzzle.

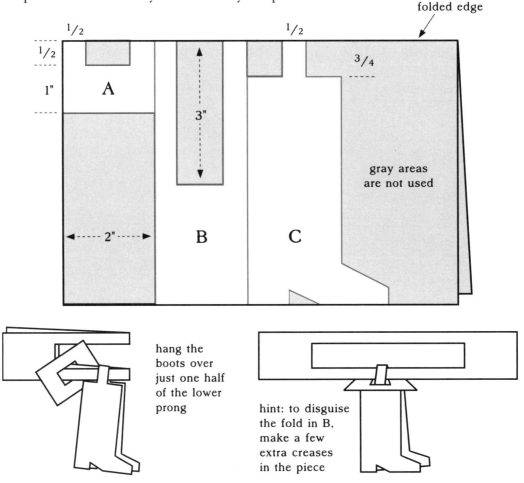

folded edge

1/2   1/2

1/2

1" A   3"

3/4

gray areas
are not used

2"   B   C

hang the boots over just one half of the lower prong

hint: to disguise the fold in B, make a few extra creases in the piece

400

THE FOUR HUNDREDTH

Starting with this puzzle's title, "The Four Hundredth," cross off letters or consecutive groups of letters as instructed. After completing the five steps, the remaining letters will spell, in order, an appropriate word.

1. Cross off a three-letter color.
2. Cross off the note on the musical scale equivalent to "fa."
3. Cross off a two-letter combination that can be added to the front of "man" or "mid" to make a five-letter word.
4. Cross off a two-letter combination that appears twice.
5. Cross off a three-letter word that precedes "Town" in a Thorton Wilder play.

End of BONUS Puzzles

Answers to these puzzles start on page 223

Once a puzzle is learned,
it can be shown to others
and, indeed, this is the
way they often give the
most amusement.

Answers
TO PUZZLES

Words and Letters

1
DOUBLE TIME

1. baaing, bazaar, ma'am
2. highhanded, hitchhike, bathhouse, beachhead, fishhawk, fishhook, roughhewn, roughhouse, washhouse, withhold
3. genii, radii, shiitake, skiing, taxiing (as in: taxiing down a runway)
4. bookkeeper, chukker, jackknife, knickknack, lockkeeper (on a canal), trekked
5. muumuu, vacuum
6. chivvy, civvies, divvy, flivver, revved, savvy, skivvies
7. arrowwood, arrowworm, bowwow, glowworm, plowwright, powwow screwworm, yellowwood

2
WHAT'S THE WORD?

The word is "inland" — the letter "l" in the middle, "in" the beginning, "and" at the end.

3
NO SEE NO SAW

No one saw it was on backwards.

4
BURIED PROVERB

A rolling stone gathers no moss.

5
THE ABSURD WORD

The word is "senselessness."

6
Q QUIZ

1. quiet
2. queue
3. quail
4. quasi
5. quake
6. quack
7. quill
8. query
9. queer
10. quite
11. queen
12. quirk
13. quota
14. quote
15. quaff
16. quest
17. quick
18. quilt
19. quart
20. quads
21. qualm
22. Queeg
23. quips
24. quell or quash

7
THE TEN WORDS

"Mispelled" is misspelled.

8
I SEE A LOT OF THAT

That that is, is. That that is not, is not. That that is is not that that is not. That that is not is not that that is. Is that not so? It is.

9
HAD ENOUGH?

John, where James had had "had," had had "had had"; "had had" had had a better effect on the teacher.

The two boys were evidently writing compositions, and from the looks of things their teacher preferred the use of "had had."

10
ER...WHAT DOES IT SAY?

bigger and bolder

11
BEHEADINGS

1. slack-lack
2. ledge-edge
3. creed-reed
4. ozone-zone
5. their-heir
6. thump-hump

12
CAN YOU READ IT?

I understand you undertake to overthrow my undertaking.

13
GHOTI

The answer is "fish." GH is pronounced "f" as in "enough," O is pronounced "i" as in "women," and TI is pronounced "sh" as in "attention."

14
THE FOUR ADJECTIVES

Tremendous, hazardous, horrendous, stupendous. There are a number of more obscure answers, the most common of which is "jeopardous."

15
ARE YOU SAGE?

Corsage, dosage, dressage, envisage, massage, message, passage, presage, sagebrush, sageness, sages, sausage, spousage, usage, visage.

Osage is also acceptable and give yourself credit if you got "newsagent" (mostly British usage).

16
LITTLE WORDS
FROM BIG ONES

No answer

17
HOW'S YOUR SPANISH?

1. Los Angeles 2. Palo Alto 3. Santa Fe
4. Florida 5. Nevada

18
THE WORD PYRAMID

One of the possible answers is as follows:

19
FOUR-LETTER PUZZLE

deny (eeny is also acceptable)

20
THE MISSING LETTER PUZZLE

The missing letter is "a." The solution is:

What mars a land so sadly as a war?
   What days as dark as days that war
   alarm?
Alas! ask any, ask at hand, afar,
   All shall call war a harass and a harm.
Why call, as ballads talk, that ghastly art
   All gallant acts — a grand and manly
   part.

21
ALPHABET SENTENCES

Here are three sentences that contain all the letters of the alphabet, the first of which is the shortest, containing 32 letters.

Pack my box with five dozen liquor jugs.
The quick brown fox jumps over a lazy dog.
It was exquisitely deep blue just then, with filmy clouds over it, like gauze.

22
BURIED POETS

The poets are Gray, Moore, Byron, Pope, Dryden, Gay, Keats, and Donne.

23
CONCEALED LETTERS

There are 13 straight-lined letters:
E F H I K L M N T V X Y Z

24
WORD ENIGMAS

Ontario (on "TA" — "RIO")
undertones (under "T" — one "S")

25
ABC-TUMBLE DOWN D

"Abie, see de cuties?"
"Oh, 'em ain' no cuties?"
"Oh, 'es, 'ey are, Abie, see 'em?"
"Oh, gee, I see 'em."
"'Es, 'ey are Ellen, Elsie, and Eloise!"

26
ANIMAL KINGDOM

1. be, bee
2. bare, bear
3. dough, doe
4. dear, deer
5. flee, flea
6. hoarse, horse
7. knew, gnu
8. taper, tapir
9. row, roe
10. you, ewe
11. links, lynx
12. hair, hare
13. burred, bird
14. earn, ern or erne
15. burrow, burro
16. mewl, mule
17. faun, fawn
18. coarser, courser*
19. weather, wether*

*A courser is swift horse; a wether is a neutered ram.

27
WHAT'S THIS?

nothing after all

28
SPELLING BEE

Here's our list. Nice going if you found others.

abstemious
angst
anvil
bang
barn
canst
diet
dime
gnarl
grab
hulk
hurl

husk
lied
lime
lush
pied
piety
plié
plied
plush
pour
rang
rush

snarl
stem
stye
stymie
stymied
vied

29
THE YY SENTENCE

Too wise you are, too wise you be;
I see you are too wise for me.

30
THE PROFESSOR'S PUZZLE

TO TIE MULES TO — The letters of the words were broken to fit on the narrow stone.

31
ONE-LETTER WORDS

1. P (pea)
2. T (tea)
3. C (sea)
4. G (gee)
5. I (eye)
6. O (owe)
7. D (Dee)
8. L (ell)
9. J (jay)
10. K (Kay)
11. R (are)
12. Q (cue)
13. B (bee)
14. U (you!)

32
TWO-LETTER WORDS

1. IC (icy)
2. XS (excess)
3. DK (decay)
4. EZ (easy)
5. MT (empty)
6. SA (essay)
7. CD (seedy)
8. XL (excel)
9. AT (eighty)
10. FX (effects)
11. NV (envy)
12. TP (tepee)

33
MORE-LETTER WORDS

1. XTC (ecstasy)   3. NRG (energy)
2. NME (enemy)   4. XPDNC
                      (expediency)

34
THE TYPEWRITER'S TOP ROW

perpetuity, proprietor, repertoire

35
WORD MAKING

1. age, are, art, ate, ear, eat, era, erg, eta, gar, get, rag, rat, tag, tar, tea; ager, gate, gear, rage, rate, tare, tear
2. evil, live, veil, vile
3. skate, stake, steak, takes, teaks
4. opts, post, pots, spot, stop, tops
5. arts, pars, part, past, pats, prat, raps, rapt, rasp, rats, spar, spat, star, taps, tarp, trap, tsar; parts, prats, strap, tarps, traps
6. a single word

36
WORD GROWING PAINS

a, at, ate, rate, crate, create, cremate
a, ad, and, land, laned, planed, planned
I, in, sin, sing, swing, sewing, stewing, strewing

37
WORD ENIGMAS

A. piano   B. stocking   C. problem
D. planet

38
LETTER ADDING

A. ail   B. east   C. ought   D. eat

39
ANIMAL ADDITIONS

1. elephant (ell + F + ant)
2. monkey (monk + key)
3. heron (hair + in)
4. chipmunk (chip + monk)
5. pony (Po + knee)
6. scorpion (score + pea + on)
7. porcupine (pork + yew + pine)
8. katydid (Katy + did)
9. hedgehog (hedge + hog)

40
WORD ADDITIONS

1. fortunate (for + tune + 8)
2. highway (hi + weigh)
3. ocean (oh + shin)
4. fortify (four + tea + fie)
5. sincere (sin + sear)

41
WORD SUBTRACTIONS

1. measured - sure = mead
2. cheap - he = cap
3. bride - rid = be
4. frankly - rank = fly
5. wearing - ear = wing

42
EASY DOES IT

ROBIN

43
FORWARD AND BACKWARD

1. live-evil
2. laid-dial
3. pans-snap
4. sleep-peels
5. parts-strap
6. tort-trot
7. snug-guns
8. golf-flog
9. star-rats
10. tins-snit

44
WORD TRANSFORMATIONS

Variations are possible for some of these.

1. east, last, lest, west
2. boy, bay, ban, man
3. hate, have, lave, love
4. hard, hart, hast, east, easy
5. heat, head, held, hold, cold
6. walk, balk, bark, mark, mart, tart, tort, toot, trot
7. silk, sink, sins, sans, sags, rags
8. dust, must, mast, mash, wash
9. take, tale, tall, tail, jail
10. slow, slot, soot, moot, most, mast, fast
11. sail, said, slid, slip, ship
12. white, whine, shine, spine, spice, slice, slick, slack, black
13. dawn, darn, dark
14. moon, soon, soot, spot, spat, spar, star
15. rich, rice, ride, rode, role, pole, poll, pool, poor
16. dry, cry, coy, cot, lot, let, wet
17. rain, raid, said, slid, slit, slot, slow, snow
18. moth, mote, more, mire, fire
19. bird, bard, ward, wand, wind, wing
20. here, hare, care, cane, cone, gone

45
PUNCTUATION PUZZLES

1. Were "but" but "and," and "and" but "but," "but" and "and" would be "and" and "but."
2. This one contains a catch because the conversation concerns the pronunciation of the name Said in Egypt, which is pronounced "Sah-eed":
I said, "I said you said I said Said." He said, "Who said I said you said Said? I said, Said is not said like 'said'."

46
GUESS THE WORDS

1. Livid has all those meanings.
2. murmur
3. one word
4. heroine
5. There are several. One is "needles," which becomes "needless" when an "s" is added.

47
GEOGRAPHICAL BURIALS

1. Salem
2. Bogota
3. Toledo
4. Spain
5. Berlin
6. Paris
7. Cuba
8. Butte
9. Canada
10. Siam, Thailand

48
RE-WORD IT

The words are rearranged as follows:

```
W A T E R
  T E N O R
  A D D E R
  S E N O R
    O T T E R
```

The seven words reading down are: at, tea, ends, rodeo, rent, rot, and re

49
WORD CHARADE

Alabama

50
NUMBERS AND LETTERS

1. ten + d = tend
2. one + n = none
3. four + l = flour
4. eight + w = weight
5. seven - s = even
6. three - r = thee
7. four - u = fur

51
ANOTHER SPELLING BEE

Here's our list. Nice going if you found others.

acknowledging	pack
akin	puck
caking	quack
edging	quaking
glow	skin
jowl	skua
king	tole
knot	town
know	wedging
ledging	wing
lewd	wink
muck	wont
mucky	zing

52
DO U KNOW IT?

unite, untie

53
NOUN AND VERB

1. purse
2. box
3. pack
4. throw
5. show
6. hide

54
A WELL-SCRAMBLED PROVERB

He who laughs last, laughs best.
or: He laughs best who laughs last.

Matchsticks

55
WHAT ARE MATCHES MADE OF?

Most people will try, and nearly succeed at, spelling the word "WOOD." The correct answer, however, involves the substance of a different kind of match altogether — love. (We've separated the letters slightly to more clearly illustrate the solution.)

56
THE THREE SQUARES

57
6 PLUS 5 EQUALS 9

58
FROM 6 TO 3

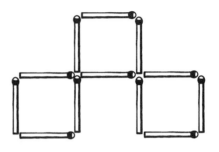

59
FROM 6 TO 2

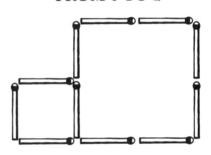

60
FROM 9 TO 2

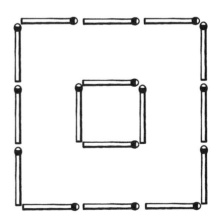

61
THE BRIDGE OF MATCHES

Here's a view from above. In case you're doubtful — it does works! However, you may need another set of hands to get the matches arranged properly.

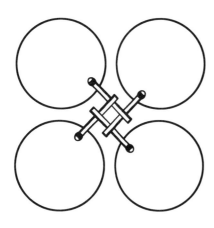

63
THREE DIFFERENT SHAPES

The three shapes are illustrated at right, slightly separated to better define them.

64
OVERLAPPING SQUARES

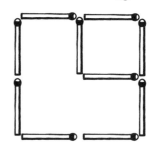

62
FROM FALSE TO TRUE

The first answer:
1 equals the square root of 1

The second answer:
11 (in Arabic numerals) equals
11 (in Roman numerals)

65
TAKE AWAY 2
AND LEAVE 2

66
TAKE AWAY 3
AND LEAVE 10

67
TAKE AWAY 1
AND LEAVE 1

68
THE 10 PUZZLE

69
THE 10 X 10 PUZZLE

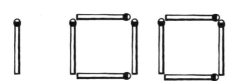

70
FOUR TRIANGLES

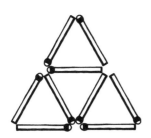

71
BIG AND LITTLE SQUARES

72
FROM 9 TO 5

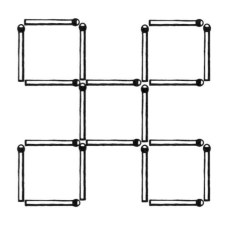

73
FROM 4 TO 2

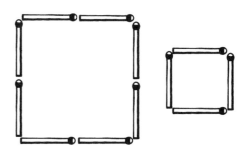

74
MATCH TRIANGLES

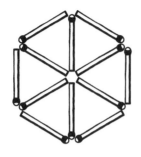

75
FROM 4 TO 3

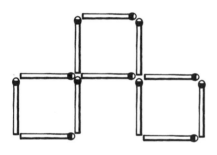

76
5 MAKES 19

Many people will try to make the figure "19." The correct answer, however, is accomplished using Roman numerals.

Wrong   Right!

   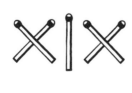

77
THE TWO DIAMONDS

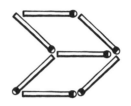

78
FROM 7 TO 5

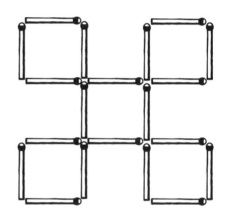

79
FROM 5 TO 4

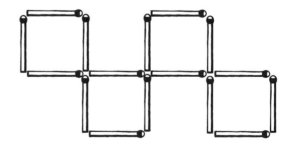

80

THE TRICKY PUZZLE

1. Remove matches A, B, C, and D and put them to one side for a moment.
2. This will leave you with the arrangement shown in diagram 2.
3. Slide E to the right and F to the left.
4. Form the 3rd square using A, B, C, and D.

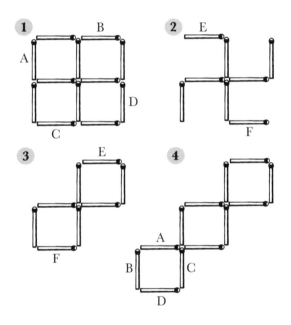

81

THE THREE-MATCH SQUARE

Here's how you will make "it" with only three matches:

82

FROM 8 TO 3

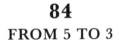

83

THE LAST MATCH

The first thing to do is make sure your opponent goes first. Then, on each of your turns, select matches so that you leave 13, then 9, then 5, and then 1 match on the table. You can't lose!

84

FROM 5 TO 3

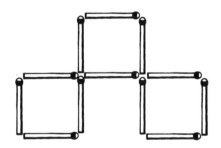

85
GUARDS AND PRISONERS

1. Two guards cross in the boat, one comes back.
2. One guard and one prisoner cross, the guard comes back.
3. One guard and one prisoner cross, the guard comes back.
4. One guard and one prisoner cross, the guard comes back.
5. Two guards cross.

86
TRIANGLE TROUBLE

87
TRICKY 20

First arrange the matches to form the Roman numeral XIX, or 19 (XXI will also work). Then remove the "I" in the middle.

88
THREE AND A HALF DOZEN

This is solved by putting three matches in one pile and the remaining six in another. You then have three — and a half dozen.

89
BING CROSBY'S MATCH PUZZLE

90
SQUARES AND TRIANGLES

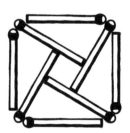

91
TRIANGLE BUILDING

This is a 3-dimensional pyramid.

92
SQUARE TRIANGLE BUILDING

This is the 3-dimensional structure.

93
THE SWIMMING FISH

The light gray matches show the original positions.

94
NO SQUARES

Here's one solution:

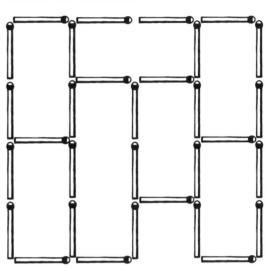

Brain Twisters

95
WEIGHT LIFTING

The weight traveled up and down a total of 55 feet. It was raised ten feet four times (40 feet) and slipped back five feet three times (15 feet). This can easily be worked out by tracing its course on a piece of paper.

96
THE BAR OF SILVER

He cut the bar into five pieces, representing $1/30$, $2/30$, $4/30$, $8/30$, and $15/30$ of the total. Then by giving and trading pieces already given, he could keep the employee paid up to date. On the first day he gave him the $1/30$ piece. On the second day he gave him the $2/30$ piece and took back the $1/30$ piece. On the third day he gave him back the $1/30$ piece to go with the $2/30$ piece, and so on.

97
DOUBLE, DOUBLE,
TOIL AND TROUBLE

The answer is 59 minutes. In effect, you're only subtracting the first minute (when the one cell doubled to two).

98
HOW MANY HAYSTACKS?

Only one. They were all piled together in the center of the field.

99
THREE CARDS

two of clubs   three of clubs   three of diamonds

100
WHAT'S YOUR NAME?

His friend was a lady and her name was Anne.

101
WHICH IS HEAVIER?

Feathers are weighed by avoirdupois weight, 16 ounces to the pound. Gold and other precious metals, however, are weighed by troy weight, 12 ounces to the pound.

102
THREE SMALL BOYS

The boy's names, let us say, were Bob, Bill, and Barney. Barney, the one who raised his hand and won the quarter, reasoned this way:

"If I do not have dirt on my forehead, then Bob and Bill raised their hands the first time because each of them saw the dirt on the other's forehead — and did not see any dirt on mine. That being so, one of them would certainly realize why the other had raised his hand the first time. Bob would know that Bill saw dirt on his forehead. Bill would know that Bob had seen dirt on his.

"If either one of them reasoned that way, he would know that he had dirt on his own forehead and would raise his hand again.

"However, since neither of them has raised his hand, that can't be the case. I must have dirt on my forehead too."

103
THE PAYCHECK PUZZLE

The answer is $123.
The product: 1 x 2 x 3 = 6
The sum: 1 + 2 + 3 = 6
The difference between the product and the sum is therefore zero. By the way, the gardener sought future employment elsewhere.

104
WHAT HAPPENED TO THE DOLLAR?

The clerk gave the bellboy $5 and kept $25. The bellboy gave each man $1 and kept $2. Each man paid $9, less $2 to the boy, leaving $25.

105
WHAT DAY?

The man went to town on Tuesday. Of the three days that the bank was open to cash his check, Tuesday was the only day when both the meat market and eye doctor's office were also open.

106
TWELVE MEN AND ELEVEN ROOMS

Read the puzzle over carefully and you will see the catch. Although it sounds otherwise, the desk clerk was still leaving one hotel guest without lodging.

Mr. Smith is the first man. After putting him to one side, he puts the second through eleventh men in rooms. When he finally deals with Mr. Smith, putting him in the last room, the twelfth man is still without a room.

107
WHO'S WHO ON
THE BALL TEAM?

Many of the details in this puzzle are unimportant, serving merely as a way of establishing who a certain player isn't. For example, the fact that Joe and the third baseman live in the same building isn't a factor in solving the puzzle (the first statement), but it does tell you that Joe isn't the third baseman, which is very helpful.

Pitcher: Joe
Catcher: Harry
First: Bob
Second: Jim
Shortstop: Bill
Third: Ed
Left: Jack
Center: Frank
Right: Tom

108
WHAT A FAMILY

There are two daughters and two sons now. With another son, each daughter would have one sister and three brothers.

109
NOON AND SUNSET

It doesn't have to be a city in California. Actually, at noon, the Sun is that much closer to any place on Earth in comparison to its position at sunset.

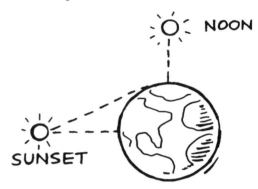

110
EGG BOILING

Three minutes when boiled in three separate pots.

111
WHAT KIND OF BILLS?

He had one $50 bill, a $5 bill, and four $2 bills (which have gone in and out of use over the years).

112
WHO'S THE OFFICER?

The third prisoner was lying and therefore was the officer. The second prisoner's statement must have been true. If it were false, both he and the first prisoner would be officers — but there was only one officer.

113
THE SIGNPOST

The signpost had three pointers. He set it up so the pointer bearing the name of the town he had just come from pointed along the road from that town.

114
FAMILY PARTY

The party consisted of two little boys and two little girls, their mother and father, and both their mother's and father's parents — the children's two grandfathers and two grandmothers.

115
ALONE, ALONE, ALL ALL ALONE

The young man married the mother of his father's second wife and had a son. His stepmother also had a son. The young man was, therefore, the husband of his father's mother-in-law, the father of his stepbrother's nephew and the father-in-law of his stepmother. It might also be conceded that he is his own grandfather.

116
HOW MANY SPARES?

They would need two spares, not four, as many are apt to guess. At the end of 6,000 miles the two spares are put on the rear wheels. They last out the remaining 12,000 miles. At the end of 12,000 miles, the front tires are done for and are replaced by the tires previously removed from the rear wheels.

117
THE ANT'S PATH

The best way to see for yourself is to draw a diagram of the room like the one shown below. This can be cut out and folded together in the shape of the room if you like. The dotted line shows the shortest possible route, which is 40 feet long. Note that the ant crosses the ceiling, back wall, and the floor on the way to his destination.

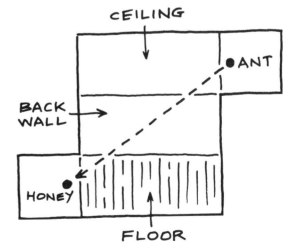

118
THE LEAKY BAG

She started out with $45. She spent $22 for the lamp, $10 for the frame, $4 for the pincushions, and $1 for the nail file.

119
AN ODD MARRIAGE

The young woman's father married the sister of the man to whom his daughter was married.

120
WHO HAS HOW MUCH?

Mrs. Stevens: $9,000
Mrs. Smith: $7,500
Mrs. Jones: $6,000
Mrs. Brown: $4,500
Mrs. Carr: $3,000
Mrs. Rose: $1,500

121
THE SIX COLLEGE MEN

Bob goes to Dartmouth.
John goes to Yale.
Sam goes to Harvard.
Rich goes to Columbia.
Harry goes to Princeton.
Martin goes to Cornell.

122
WHAT COLOR WAS THE BEAR?

White. It was a polar bear, because the men set up their camp on the North Pole. That is the only place from which they could walk ten miles south, then ten miles west and be at a point exactly ten miles from where they started.

123
DINNER OUT

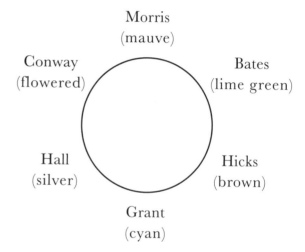

Morris (mauve)
Conway (flowered)
Bates (lime green)
Hall (silver)
Hicks (brown)
Grant (cyan)

124
FUNNY TRAVELER

Bill is an elevator operator in the Empire State Building in New York City. He makes two trips every four minutes to the 80th floor and back — a distance of 2,000 feet. During a eight-hour day this works out to 180,000 feet or 45.5 miles.

125
TARGET PRACTICE

He took six shots. Two landed on 16 and four on 17.

126
WINE AND WATER

It is hard to believe, but there are equal amounts of water and wine in the two glasses.

Assume that each glass contained 100 units of liquid and that the spoon held 10 units. The spoon first removes 10 units of water, so the water glass contains 90 units of water, and the wine glass contains 100 units of wine and 10 units of water.

With 110 units in the wine glass, the spoon will remove 1/11 of each liquid in that glass. Thus, it will transfer to the water glass 9 1/11 units of wine and 10/11 units of water. The water glass will then contain 90 10/11 units of water and 9 1/11 units of wine, and the wine glass will contain 90 10/11 units of wine and 9 1/11 units of water.

127
HOW FAR TO DUNHAM?

The distance was 60 miles, he rode at 12 m.p.h., and the appointment was at 5:00.

If the man left Dedham at noon and rode for four hours at 15 m.p.h., he would reach Dunham at 4:00, an hour too soon.

If he rode at 10 m.p.h., he would arrive at 6:00, an hour too late.

128
HOW OLD IS JANE?

Jane is 27 1/2 years old and Mary is 16 1/2. This will be clear if you trace the question backward, for when Mary was 5 1/2 years old, Jane was 16 1/2.

Now, when Mary is three times that age, she will be 49 1/2 years old. Half of this is 24 3/4, and when Jane was that age Mary was 13 3/4. Accordingly, Jane's age was twice this, or 27 1/2.

Just the same, it's a heck of a puzzle and a lot of people would like to lay hands on the person who invented it.

129
BUSHELS OF APPLES

He started out with 295 apples.

130
THE THREE DOORS

There are six different ways. The three women may enter the doors in any of the following combinations:

1	2	3
1	3	2
2	1	3
2	3	1
3	1	2
3	2	1

131
WHO'S THAT MAN?

"That man" is the son of the person speaking.

132
RISING TIDE

The first three rungs will never be covered with water for the ship and the ladder will rise with the tide.

133
THE LYING ARCHEOLOGIST

The maker of the coin would never have known that it was B.C. This symbol did not come into use until later.

134
THE NUTS AND BOLTS JOB

The one who wanted the $3,000/year raise would be cheaper. Over a three-year period, he would receive $54,000 vs. the other applicant, who would make $56,250.

1. $15,000 + $18,000 + $21,000
2. $7,500 ($1/2$ year) + $8,250 + $9,000 + $9,750 + $10,500 + $11,250

135
THE TWO "OUT" PROVERB

Out of sight, out of mind.

136
THE PICNIC

It was a threesome — a grandmother, mother, and daughter.

137
THE TWO COINS

This is a trick question. One of the coins is not a nickel, it is a 50-cent piece. The other coin, however, is a nickel.

138
THE BRIDGE GAME

Table A: Mrs. Allen, Mrs. Dewey, Mr. Cole, Mr. Bing

Table B: Mr. Allen, Mr. Dewey, Mrs. Bing, Mrs. Cole

139
THREE TRAVELERS

At first sight it would seem that the money should be divided according to the bread furnished. However, since the three men ate a total of eight loaves, each man ate $2 2/3$ loaves.

Subtracting $2 2/3$ from the five loaves the first traveler brought would mean he furnished the third traveler with $2 1/3$ loaves.

Subtracting $2 2/3$ from the three loaves the second traveler brought means he furnished the third traveler with $1/3$ of a loaf.

$2 1/3$ to $1/3$, or 7 to 1, is the ratio in which the money is to be divided.

140
A BATH FOR THE JINX

He pulled the plug of the bathtub and let the water run out. Of course, that solved only his drowning problem.

141
THE CARPENTER'S PUZZLE

The carpenter made the first two cuts as represented by A and B.

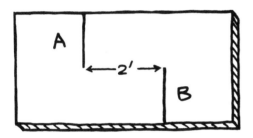

142
THE SIX SHOPPERS

Mrs. Smith: rug/first floor
Mrs. Brown: dress/second
Mrs. Deeds: hat/second
Mrs. Jones: book/third
Mrs. Mann: shoes/fourth
Mrs. Gregory: lamp/fifth

143
FOX, DUCK AND
A BAG OF CORN

He first took the duck across the river. Then he took the fox across and brought the duck back. Next, he took the corn across. Then he returned alone and brought the duck across.

144
FAMILY MIX-UP

Three. They are the widower's first wife, the widower himself, and his second wife. The usual reaction is to think that the widower's second wife is also a widow and, therefore, that her first husband is also part of the mix-up.

145
THE KIND FATHER'S DEAL

These boys thought they were pretty smart. Each one drove the other's car. As a consequence, the brother in the car that came in first won the fortune, since his own car was left behind and came in last.

146
PICK THE WINNER

Moonlight was the winner, one length ahead of Daytime, three lengths ahead of Star and Swift, six lengths ahead of Sunbeam, and seven lengths ahead of Planet.

147
HOBSON'S CHOICE

The prisoner said: "I will jump off the cliff into the bottomless gorge."

148
NO CHANGE

He had a 50-cent piece, a quarter, and four dimes.

149
FAMILY RELATIONSHIPS

1. niece or daughter
2. great-grandmother
3. great-aunt
4. son or nephew
5. stepfather
6. brother-in-law
7. yourself
8. first cousin
9. grandmother
10. mother
11. stepmother

150
THE PAWN SHOP SWAP

Mr. Sniggers was the gullible party who lost. He overlooked the fact that he would have to pay $4 to the pawnbroker to redeem the $5 bill. Thus he paid $8 for the $5 bill and lost $3.

151
TOO MANY GIRLS

There were five boy-girl couples, the same number as that of the extra girls.

152
A TANGLED DEAL

Tammy lost 60 cents, made up of the 40 cents Betty owed her and the 20 cents she paid Betty. Tammy kept the vase, which was worth 75 cents, so did not lose anything by that part of the deal.

153
THE HORSE THIEF

Joseph took Jim's horse.

First, let's figure out the thief:

1. The first statement makes it clear that John's brother is the horse thief. Therefore John is not guilty.
2. Jack cannot be John's brother since he has met John's father only once. Therefore Jack is not guilty.
3. Jim, the trip's arranger, is willing to finger the thief. Therefore Jim is not guilty.
4. So Joseph is the horse thief.

Now for the victim:

1. Joseph is the thief, so obviously he's not the victim.
2. John was on his horse when he met the sheriff, so he's not the victim.
3. This leaves Jim and Jack. Since Jack and Joseph have know John for only five days, they didn't customarily play golf with John. Consequently, one of them must have eaten with the victim on the night before they set out on the trip. Since Joseph had been out of town, it wasn't him. Therefore Jack ate with the victim. Since Joseph and John were already eliminated, the victim was Jim.

154
THE MYSTERIOUS ORDER

The Sad Sack had been sleeping while he was on duty.

155
THE CUBES

1. six
2. twenty-seven
3. none
4. eight
5. twelve
6. six
7. one

156
BIG AND LITTLE CLIMBER

The big climber was the little climber's mother.

157
DROPS OF WATER

During the seventh hour. At the end of that hour the glass would have received 56 drops, just over half of the 110-drop total at the end of ten hours.

158
THE CHECKERS TOURNAMENT

First: John Black
Second: Bob White
Third: Rob Roy
Fourth: Jim Black

Here's how to figure it:

Statement four states that the runner-up didn't attend college, so it couldn't have been either of the Blacks. It also states that the runner-up isn't married. Since statement five mentions Rob Roy's wedding, Bob White must have finished second.

Since Rob Roy was beaten by Bob White, he finished third or fourth. Statement three makes it obvious that the third place finisher had never met the winner, and the Black brothers had obviously met each other, so Rob Roy was third.

So which Black won and which was fourth? Statement three shows that the winner hadn't met the third place finisher (Rob Roy). Since Jim Black had been an usher at Rob Roy's wedding, John Black must have been the winner.

159
LINES AND SQUARES

Most people will figure that nine small squares are formed. This is correct, but in addition there is the one large square containing the others and four medium-sized squares, each composed of four of the small squares. The answer therefore is 14 squares.

160
LINK BY LINK

Beatrice cut the third link, leaving a single link (the third), a two-link section, and a four-link section. She paid the single link the first day. The second day she paid the two-link section and took back the single link. On the third day she paid the single link. On the fourth day she paid the four-link section and took back the single link and the two-link section. Then she started again with the single link, as on the first day and carried through as on the first three days.

161
THE HUNDRED COINS

There was one 50-cent piece, 39 dimes, and 60 pennies.

162
CUT THE PIE

First, make a circular cut around the center of the pie. Then make two straight cuts through the center.

163
WHO WAS THE PICCOLO PLAYER?

Little Bill.

According to the second statement, Little Bill wasn't the piano player. Therefore, either Little Bob or Little Ben was the piano player. Either Big Bill or Big Ben pitched horseshoes, because Big Bob didn't play games or sports. That rules out Little Bob as the pianist, because the pianist's father pitched horseshoes. Little Ben, therefore, played the piano.

Now, according to the first statement, Little Bob could not be the piccolo player, for Big Bob never played games or sports and so wouldn't play ball with his son. Little Bob was not the pianist, nor was he the piccolo player, so he must have played the violin. By elimination, it was Little Bill who played the piccolo.

164
MORE FAMILY RELATIONSHIPS

William is Walter's grandfather.

165
THE POKER PLAYERS

Bill exchanged his $5.10 for Jim's quarter and was square. Then Jim gave $1.50 to Walter in exchange for Walter's 85 cents. After Bill and Walter went home, Jim gave Harry the $5.95 he then had, took Harry's $4.55, and they were all even.

166
FILLING THE PEACH BASKET

It was half full at the end of five minutes.

167
A TWISTER TO END ALL TWISTERS

Frankly, this one is almost too much to bear, but here goes:

The answer is Tuesday. It figures out as follows: What is today (Tuesday) if, when the day after tomorrow (Thursday) is yesterday (this brings us to Friday), today (Friday) will be as far from Tuesday (three days) as today (this time referring to a new and different today) was from Tuesday when the day before yesterday (Sunday, in relation to the original to-day) was tomorrow (meaning Saturday). Counting forward, Saturday is three days from Tuesday, as, counting backward, Friday is three days from it.

168
TUG OF WAR

The 37th minute. At the 36th minute the Black team was two inches away from the line. A loss of three inches in the next minute would put them over, ending the contest.

169
THE CLOCK'S HANDS

Eleven times at 1:05, 2:11, 3:16, 4:22, and so on.

170
THE THREE VERSATILE MEN

Harold: painter and musician
Henry: lawyer and merchant
Herbert: banker and writer

1. Harold must have been the painter (sixth statement).
2. Henry couldn't have been the writer (fifth statement) and Harold couldn't have been the writer (second statement), so the writer was Herbert.
3. Henry is then the merchant (second statement).

Continuing from there:

4. The banker wasn't Harold, the painter (fourth statement), and the banker wasn't Henry, the merchant (first statement), so the banker was Herbert.
5. The lawyer wasn't Harold, the painter (third statement), and the lawyer wasn't Herbert, because he was the writer and banker, so the lawyer was Henry.
6. By elimination, the musician must have been Harold.

171
A FINGER IN THE WATER

Your finger displaces an amount of water equal to the size and weight of the finger. Therefore, the glass of water will be heavier by the weight of two inches of finger.

Numbers

172
MULTIPLE MIX-UP

When you multiply 142,857 by any of the numbers 1–6, you get the same series of numbers, though shifted slightly. For example, 2 x 142,857 is 285,714, with the "14" removed from the front and tacked onto the end. Likewise, 3 x 142,857 is 428,571, with the "1" shifted to the rear.

Whatever one number your friend tells you, simply write it down and then fill in the surrounding letters in their proper order.

To figure out the multiplier, look at the right-hand number in your friend's result. Since the right-hand number in 142,857 is 7, if your friend's result ends in 4, you know the multiplier was 2. That's because only 2 x 7 will give you that last number of 4. If your friend's result ends in 1, the multiplier was 3. A result ending in 8, 5, or 2 means, respectively, a multiplier of 4, 5, or 6.

173
THE NINES PUZZLE

The answer is 20. Most people will count 9, 19, 29, and so on up to 99 and give the answer as 10, completely forgetting about 90, 91, 92, and the rest of the 90's. And don't forget that 99 has two 9's.

174
FROM 45 TO 100

The new formula is:
$1 + 2 + 3 + 4 + 5 + 6 + 7 + (8 \times 9)$

175
A NUMBER ENIGMA

The answer is LOVE. L is 50, O is 0, V is 5, and E is 1/8 of "EIGHT."

176
FUNNY DIVISION

Start by writing 12 in Roman numerals: XII. Crossing off the bottom half of that leaves VII.

177
HOW MANY NUMBERS?

There are six combinations: 123, 132, 213, 231, 312, and 321

178
NINE-DIGIT NUMBERS

Here's the equation and answer. The answer's unique feature is that it also contains all the digits 1–9:

$$\begin{array}{r} 9\,8\,7\,6\,5\,4\,3\,2\,1 \\ -\,1\,2\,3\,4\,5\,6\,7\,8\,9 \\ \hline 8\,6\,4\,1\,9\,7\,5\,3\,2 \end{array}$$

179
THE FOUR PUZZLE

The answer is 5 $1/3$.

180
FIND THE NUMBER

The number is 120. It is equal to one-half the sum of these numbers, which are its exact divisors: 1, 2, 3, 4, 5, 6, 8, 10, 12, 15, 20, 24, 30, 40, and 60. Those numbers add up to 240.

181
ANOTHER OF THE SAME KIND

The number is 672. It is equal to one-half the sum of its exact divisors, which are: 1, 2, 3, 4, 6, 7, 8, 12, 14, 16, 21, 24, 28, 32, 42, 48, 56, 84, 96, 112, 168, 224, and 336.

182
TWICE AND THRICE

There are three correct solutions:
219, 438, and 657
192, 384, and 576
273, 546, and 819

183
ONE ALONE

The solution uses two fractions that both equal $1/2$:

$148/296 + 35/70 = 1$

184
FOUR FIVES

55 $5/5$

185
MAGIC MULTIPLICATION

The pattern holds up for each example up to and including 9.

186
THE ONE-HALF PUZZLE

7,293/14,586 and 7,329/14,658

187
THE ONE-THIRD PUZZLE

5,823/17,469

188
MISSING NUMBERS

Addition:

$$\begin{array}{r} 292 \\ 7042 \\ +\ 3279 \\ \hline 10613 \end{array}$$

Multiplication:

$$\begin{array}{r} 4876 \\ \times\ 327 \\ \hline 1594452 \end{array}$$

Subtraction:

$$\begin{array}{r} 8756 \\ -\ 3980 \\ \hline 4776 \end{array}$$

189
WHEN SUBTRACTION MEANS ADDITION

The puzzle is solved by using Roman numerals. Take away I (1) from XXIX (29) and you're left with XXX (30).

190
THE 48 PUZZLE

Divide 48 into 42 and 6.
$42 \div 6 = 7$
$6 \div 3 = 2$
$7 + 2 = 9$

191
THE EIGHT 8'S

$888 + 88 + 8 + 8 + 8 = 1,000$

192
ADDING AND MULTIPLYING

Many people would solve such a problem reading left to right, which would give an answer of 0 (since any number multiplied by 0 is 0). However, using proper math rules, where multiplications are performed before additions, the correct answer is 10.

193
MAGIC SQUARE OF 15

The numbers in the left and right columns can be swapped:

8	1	6
3	5	7
4	9	2

194
MAGIC SQUARE OF 34

16	2	3	13
5	11	10	8
9	7	6	12
4	14	15	1

195
MAGIC SQUARE OF 65

17	24	1	8	15
23	5	7	14	16
4	6	13	20	22
10	12	19	21	3
11	18	25	2	9

196
MAGIC SQUARE OF 111

35	1	6	26	19	24
3	32	7	21	23	25
31	9	2	22	27	20
8	28	33	17	10	15
30	5	34	12	14	16
4	36	29	13	18	11

197
CROSSED-OUT NUMBERS

After crossing out the proper numbers, you will have left the equation shown here; which, if a zero is assumed after the two nines in the bottom row, add up to 1,111.

$$
\begin{array}{r}
111 \\
3 \\
7 \\
99 \\
\hline
1111
\end{array}
$$

198
THE PHILOSOPHER'S PUPILS

The answer is 28. $14 + 7 + 4 + 3 = 28$

199
THREE PLUS WHAT?

The number is 1.

200
THE 33 PUZZLE

14	7	12
9	11	13
10	15	8

201
THE 1926 PUZZLE

643	644	639
638	642	646
645	640	641

To insert your own set of consecutive numbers, begin with the solution shown in puzzle #193. By adding the same number to each cell, you will have a new puzzle that works. For example, adding 300 to each of the numbers in the first row would be: 308, 301, 306 (adding up to 915). The nine numbers used in this example would be 301–309.

202
ONE HUNDRED EVEN

$49 + 50 + 1/2 + {38}/{76} = 100$

203
THE 17 TRIANGLE

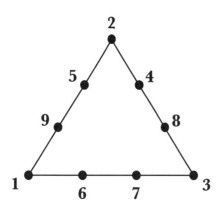

204
THE 20 TRIANGLE

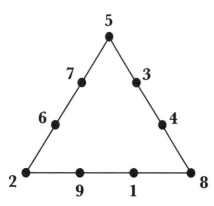

205
THE 24 PUZZLE

Solution 1: $8 + 8 + 8 = 24$
Solution 2: $22 + 2 = 24$
Solution 3: $3^3 - 3 = 24$

206
THE 41 PUZZLE

The two numbers are 1 and 41.

207
ODD TO EVEN

There are four correct answers:
$3^3/3$, $5^5/5$, $7^7/7$, and $9^9/9$

208
ONLY FOURS

The solutions using the fewest 4's (31) are as follows:

$0 = 4 - 4$
$1 = 4 \div 4$
$2 = \dfrac{(4 + 4)}{4}$
$3 = 4 - 4/4$
$4 = 4$
$5 = 4 + 4/4$
$6 = \dfrac{(4 + 4)}{4} + 4$
$7 = 44/4 - 4$
$8 = 4 + 4$
$9 = 4 + 4 + 4/4$
$10 = \dfrac{(44 - 4)}{4}$

209
THE PERFECT QUESTION

$28 = 1 + 2 + 4 + 7 + 14$

Coins

210
THREE IN A ROW

Take the white coin on the left and move it all the way to the right. Or move the right coin into the first spot. Either way, the black coin will no longer be in the middle.

211
RIGHT-ANGLE LINES

Move the bottom coin so it's atop the coin in the upper left.

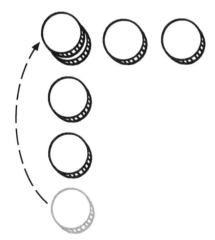

212
MOVE TO THE CENTER

Hold down the middle coin with your left index finger. With your right index finger, move the black coin to the right and then quickly back again so that it strikes the middle coin. The impact will cause the leftmost coin to slide away, creating enough room for the black coin to fit between it and the other white coin.

213
MATCHING COINS

The moved coins are shown in gray. The four lines are on a slant, which can be seen by turning your head 45 degrees to the right.

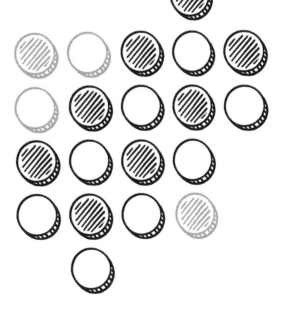

214
STAR POINTS

The only way to cover seven of the star's points is to cover, on each successive move, the point from which the previous coin started.

For example, if the first coin is moved from 1 to 6, the next move would be from 4 to 1. The remaining moves would then be 7 to 4, 2 to 7, 5 to 2, 8 to 5, and finally 3 to 8.

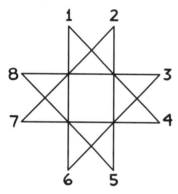

215
ALTERNATE COINS

The starting arrangement is shown, followed by the four correct moves.

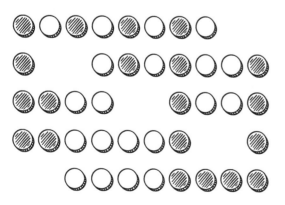

216
FIVE KINGS

The five moves are as follows:

> move 4 on 1
> move 6 on 9
> move 8 on 3
> move 2 on 5
> move 7 on 10

217
UPSIDE DOWN

218
NINE COINS IN TEN LINES

The ten lines are shown in gray.

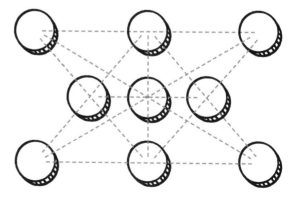

219
CHANGING PLACES

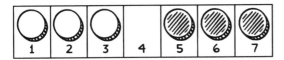

move 2 to 1
move 5 to 2
move 3 to 5
move 6 to 3
move 7 to 6
move 4 to 7
move 1 to 4
move 3 to 1
move 6 to 3
move 7 to 6

220
MORE CHANGING

move 3 to 4
move 5 to 3
move 6 to 5
move 4 to 6
move 2 to 4
move 1 to 2
move 3 to 1
move 5 to 3
move 7 to 5
move 6 to 7
move 4 to 6
move 2 to 4
move 3 to 2
move 5 to 3
move 4 to 5

221
TAILS UP

Starting with the arrangement HTH, proceed as follows:

1. Turn over the first coin, making TTH
2. Turn over the first two, making HHH
3. Turn over all three, making TTT

Alternately, the first move can be to turn over the last coin, followed by turning over the last two coins.

222
DESIGN FOR COINS

Another solution is to rotate this arrangement 90 degrees.

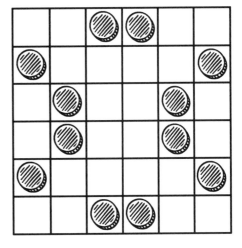

223
TWELVE LINES OF THREE

The 12 lines are shown in gray.

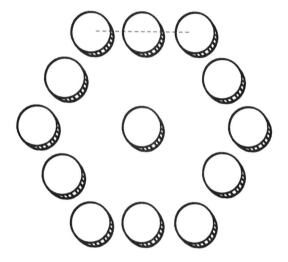

224
THE DIAMOND PENDANT

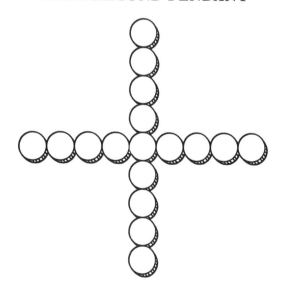

225
DOUBLING UP

The two illustrations show the starting and finishing arrangements.

There are variations on this, but here are six moves that work:

> move 12 to 3
> move 7 to 4
> move 10 to 6
> move 8 to 1
> move 9 to 5
> move 11 to 2

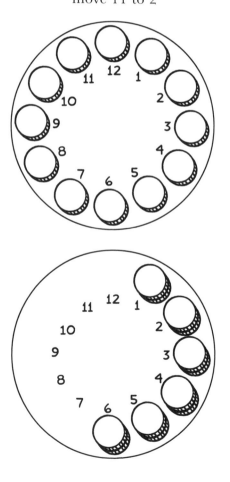

226
FOUR TO A LINE

The ten lines: the four horizontal rows, four vertical columns, and two diagonals.

227
COUNT AND TAKE OUT

Start at coin number 2 and count to 11. (If you wanted to remove all the black coins, you'd start at coin number 10 and count to 29.)

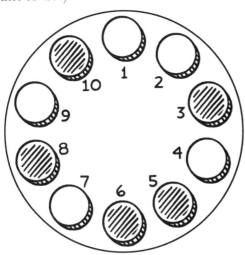

228
HEADS TO TAILS COUNTDOWN

Start with coin 2 and count to nine on each turn. This will turn over the tenth coin first, then the ninth, eighth, seventh, sixth, and so on.

The other odd numbers, 1, 3, 7, and 11 will also turn over all the coins in ten consecutive moves — although not in "countdown" order.

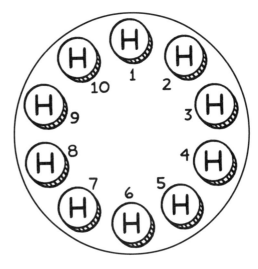

Anagrams

229
A FEW STRAIGHT ANAGRAMS

1. astronomers
2. Christianity
3. telegraph
4. Presbyterian
5. Old England

230
A MEAL OF ANAGRAMS

Tonight's Menu

Oyster soup	Red tomatoes
Boiled salmon	Roast turkey

231
WORD AND LETTER ANAGRAMS

1. ACORN plus:
   carbon, cornea, anchor, rancor
2. More of the SAME:
   seamy, shame, amuse
3. Ten more good ones:
   exert, ravage, droop, brave, blast,
   acrid, nerves, quiets, gained, gavel
4. Add two letters:
   martyr, ferret, sensation, nickel,
   parade, grafted, average, cadence,
   sublime, rancid

232
AUTHOR ANAGRAMS

Oscar Wilde, William Shakespeare

233
STATE ANAGRAMS

1. New Hampshire
2. Rhode Island
3. Minnesota
4. Pennsylvania
5. New York
6. California
7. Massachusetts
8. Nebraska

234
AN ANAGRAM DESTINATION

He was going to Constantinople, which
is spelled with the same letters as those
in "plant onions, etc."

235
ANIMALS, VEGETABLES, AND OTHERS

1. asparagus
2. cauliflower
3. artichoke
4. pineapple
5. orange
6. blueberry
7. mackerel
8. shad
9. flounder
10. elephant
11. panther
12. boa constrictor

236
GEOGRAPHICAL ANAGRAMS

1. Germany
2. Italy
3. Scotland
4. Norway
5. Portugal
6. Detroit
7. Springfield
8. Salem
9. San Francisco
10. Tallahassee

237
BY LAND AND BY SEA

Scythe, yachts

238
SCRAMBLED PROVERBS

1. Pride goeth before a fall.
2. A stitch in time saves nine.
3. Haste makes waste.
4. A rolling stone gathers no moss.
5. The early bird gets the worm.

239
SCRAMBLED POETRY

Beside the streamlet's shining band
The fisherman sat all day.
Soon he raised a lazy hand
To drive a gnat away.
Yet, though he saw me standing by,
He gave no outward sign
But kept his keen and watchful eye
Upon his slender line.

240
SCRAMBLED EGGS

1. ostrich 2. snake 3. penguin 4. tortoise
5. platypus 6. chicken 7. turkey
8. salmon 9. dinosaur 10. comedian

241
SCRAMBLED SUBJECTS

1. history 2. biology 3. geometry
4. English 5. economics 6. algebra
7. Spanish 8. physics

242
SCRAMBLED FAMOUS AMERICANS

1. Morse 2. Roosevelt 3. Sherman
4. McKinley 5. Hamilton 6. Edison
7. Monroe 8. Fulton 9. Washington
10. Grant 11. Lincoln 12. Jefferson

243
SCRAMBLED STATES

1. Oregon
2. Texas
3. Wyoming
4. Kansas
5. Iowa
6. Idaho
7. Alabama
8. New York
9. Montana
10. Arizona
11. Wisconsin
12. Vermont
13. Ohio
14. Delaware
15. Florida
16. Arkansas
17. Hawaii
18. Washington
19. Virginia
20. Utah
21. California
22. Georgia
23. Oklahoma
24. Colorado
25. Connecticut
26. Nevada
27. Maine
28. Illinois
29. Alaska
30. Mississippi
31. South Carolina
32. Tennessee
33. West Virginia
34. Indiana
35. South Dakota
36. Kentucky
37. Louisiana
38. Missouri
39. Nebraska
40. Rhode Island
41. Pennsylvania
42. North Dakota
43. North Carolina
44. Maryland
45. New Mexico
46. Massachusetts
47. Michigan
48. New Jersey
49. New Hampshire
50. Minnesota

Pencil and Paper

244
THE OLD KING'S CASTLE

The letters along the correct route spell:
THE OLD KING'S ROYAL ARMY

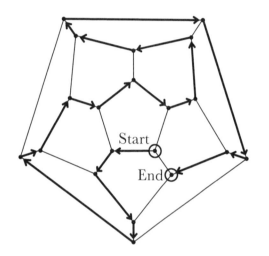

245
THE UNFRIENDLY NEIGHBORS

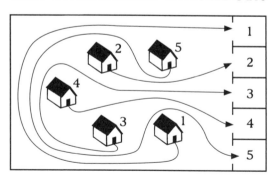

246
THE ONE-LINE ENVELOPE

Here's one
solution:

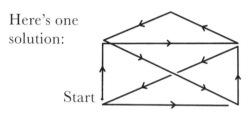

247
WATER, GAS, AND ELECTRICITY

The only way to solve the puzzle is to draw one of the lines underneath one of the houses, between the spots where the other two lines connect to that house.

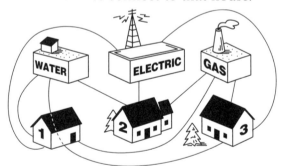

248
FOUR TURNS

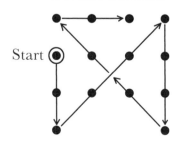

249
THE PLOT OF LAND

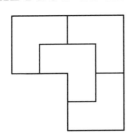

250
A BIGGER PLOT

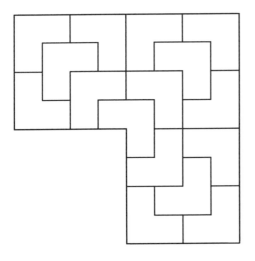

251
PENTAGON TO SQUARE

Bisect the right side and then draw lines from that point to the two corners.

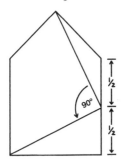

252
SHAPES AND NUMBERS

Here's one answer:

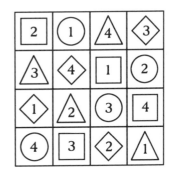

253
SWITCHING THE TRAINS

Each train is shown in two segments, uncoupled in the middle. The segments are then maneuvered in the following manner:

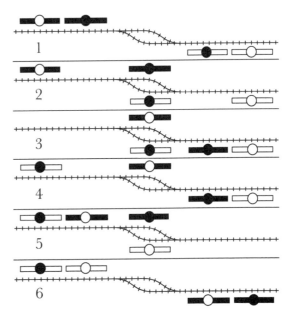

254
DOES 64 EQUAL 65?

Although the four parts appear to fit together exactly, there's a small gap along the 65-square diagonal. It's small enough that it's not really noticeable, but its area is equal to that of one of the smaller squares.

255
FOUR CURIOUS PARTS

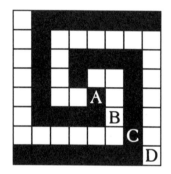

256
AROUND THE SQUARES

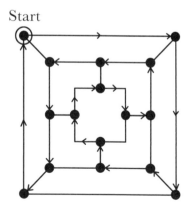

257
TRY-ANGLE

Here's one solution:

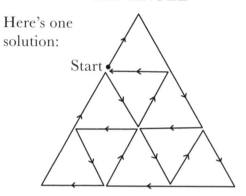

258
DOTS IN THE SQUARE

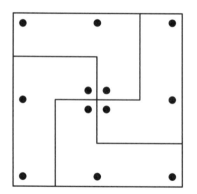

259
THE PIG PEN PUZZLE

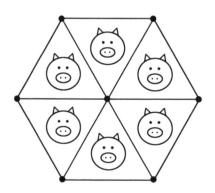

260
THREE GARDEN HOSES

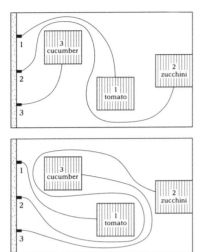

261
A HOLE IN THE BARN FLOOR

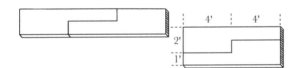

262
STAR AND CIRCLES

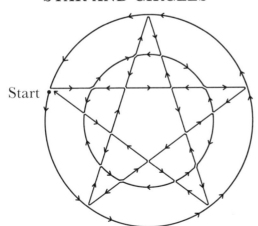

263
THE FARMER'S FENCE

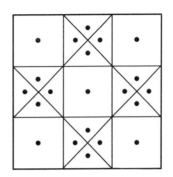

264
A HARD DIVISION

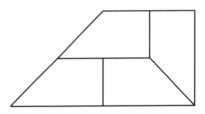

265
DIVIDING THE HEXAGON

The solution at right can be drawn by first putting in the guidelines as shown at left:

1. Connect the opposite corners.
2. Find the halfway point of each side and then connect those points.
3. Erase the extra lines.

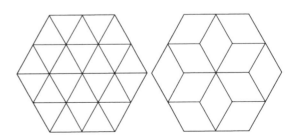

266
FOUR-SIDED DIFFICULTIES

There are 17 squares and 34 rectangles.

267
SHARE AND SHARE ALIKE

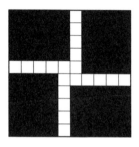

268
THE PLUS SIGN

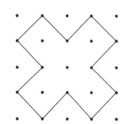

269
POINT TO POINT

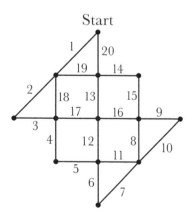

270
ROCKET SHIP OF TRIANGLES

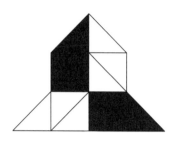

271
THE APPLE GROVE

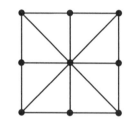

272
THREE LETTERS

The solution is shown using the letters E, L, and V to spell LEVEL. Other possibilities are: civic, deked, deled, dewed, kayak, madam, radar, refer, rotor, sagas, sexes, shahs, solos, stats, stets, and tenet. "Put up" would qualify if phrases were allowed.

L	E	V	E	L
E	E		E	E
V		V		V
E	E		E	E
L	E	V	E	L

Teasers

273
WHAT A BIRD

It's real. It's an ostrich.

274
LITTLE BODY PARTS

arm, ear, eye, gum, hip, jaw, leg, lip, rib, toe

275
FINGERS AND THUMBS

Twenty. The thumb is also a finger, as evidenced by the fact that we always speak of the ten fingers.

276
ANIMALS AT THE CIRCUS

The poor skunk's scent was a bad one.

277
THE CLOCK STRIKES

Many will say 60 seconds, but it takes 66 seconds. At 6:00 there are five intervals of six seconds each. At 12:00 there are eleven intervals of six seconds each.

278
AUGUST

Because one swift kick from the mule was the last of August.

279
THE SECOND DAY

They'll say the word "Tuesday," when the second day of the week is Monday.

280
WHAT'S IN A NAME?

The boys called the ranch "Focus" because that's where the sun's rays meet (the sons raise meat).

281
THE RIDDLE OF EUROPE

The five countries are Hungary, Italy, Germany, Norway, and Turkey, part of which is in western Asia. Vatican City is also acceptable, although it's officially an independent state.

282
WAKE UP AND GIVE

An eight-day alarm clock won't run at all unless you wind it.

283
BROTHERS AND SISTERS

Many people will say 14 — two parents, six daughters, and six brothers. The correct answer is nine since the six daughters all share the same brother.

284
DOT, DOT, DOT

hijinks, Fiji

285
NINE IN ONE

"Therein" contains these nine words: the, there, he, her, here, ere, re, rein, in

286
EYESIGHT TEST

At night. During the day, the most distant thing one can see is the sun. At night, one can see stars, which are much farther away than the sun.

287
HOLE NUMBERS

No. Holes have no dirt, they're empty.

288
THE JACKS

Twelve. Each jack has two heads.

289
STRIKE TWO

Vacate, mates

290
THE 17 EGGS

Each egg costs one cent, so 17 would cost 17 cents.

291
THE FLAG RAISING

Flags are always flown at half-mast on Memorial Day. The flag travels 150 feet — 100 feet up and then 50 feet down.

292
THE PEACOCK'S EGG

Peacocks don't lay eggs. It's the peahens that do.

293
THE EXPERIMENT

Because 80 minutes is the same amount of time as one hour and 20 minutes.

294
THE SILENT PARROT

The parrot was deaf.

295
ONE WAY OR THE OTHER

tip, pit

296
WHAT TIME WAS IT?

He entered the house on the last stroke of 12:00 midnight. That was followed by one chime at 12:30, 1:00, and 1:30.

Mathematical

297
THE NON-SHRINKING WINDOW

The window was boarded up as shown. The square is smaller, but there's no denying that it measures two feet across and two feet from top to bottom.

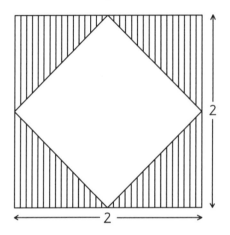

298
THE FIVE PIECES OF CHAIN

$4.50. The blacksmith takes one 3-link piece and cuts open each of its links. He then uses them to link together the other four 3-link pieces. The three cuts total $1.50 and the three welds total $3.

299
CUTTING THE POLE

It will take only ninety seconds, not one hundred seconds as many will suppose. Nine cuts will divide the pole into ten pieces.

300
AUTOMOBILE RIDE

24 miles per hour. Going to work, the man drives one mile in $1/20$ (or $3/60$) of an hour. Coming home, he drives one mile in $1/30$ (or $2/60$) of an hour. The average time per mile for the round trip is figured this way:

$$1/2 \times (3/60 + 2/60) = 5/120$$

That means it takes five hours to go 120 miles. Dividing 120 by five yields a total of 24 miles per hour.

301
BALL AND BAT

The ball cost 75 cents, the bat 50 cents.

302
FOUR GALLONS

1. Fill the three-gallon can with water and then pour it into the five-gallon can.
2. Refill the three-gallon can and pour the water from it into the five-gallon can until it is full. The three-gallon can will then contain one gallon.
3. Empty the five-gallon can and pour the three-gallon's single gallon into it.
4. Fill the three-gallon can once more and pour that into the five-gallon can. The five-gallon can will then contain four gallons.

303
THE SNAIL IN THE WELL

The 13th day. The snail's net rate is one foot a day. By the end of the 12th day, the snail will be four feet from the top. Climbing four feet on the 13th day will bring it to the top.

304
THE TWO TRAINS

Neither. When the trains meet they are at the exact same place and so are the same distance from New York.

305
HOW MANY COOKIES?

She has seven cookies to begin with. Her oldest son gets four ($3 \frac{1}{2} + \frac{1}{2}$), her middle son two, and her youngest son one.

306
HOW MANY DINNERS?

There are 5,040 arrangements (7 x 6 x 5 x 4 x 3 x 2 x 1), so the friends could eat together every evening for more than 13 years.

307
THE TWO BOOKS

$\frac{1}{2}$ inch. The worm merely ate through two covers since the first page of volume I is next to the last page of volume II.

308
THE SUITCASE OF CASH

The smallest amount the suitcase could have contained was $3,121.

309
THE HERD OF CATTLE

The farmer left 142 cows. When the neighbor added two, the 144-cow total was divided this way: 48 for the first son, 36 for the second, 24 for the third, 18 for the fourth, and 16 for the fifth.
That adds up to 142 cows.

310
THE BAND OF STEEL

Amazingly enough, the band will be nearly two inches off the earth all the way around. Furthermore, the size of the circumference makes no difference. The answer will be the same for any size band that's increased by 12 inches.

   Here's a mathematical proof for a ten-inch band. Try it for any other size band.

1. Divide ten inches by π (3.14) to get the diameter of the circle.
   Result: 3.18 inches
2. 10 + 12 inches = 22 inches ÷ 3.14
   Result: 7 inches

   That's a difference of nearly four inches in diameter, which translates to radii that differ by nearly two inches.

311
THREE MAKES 12

Here's one solution:

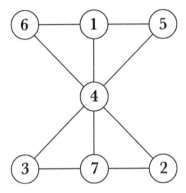

312
A HORSE DEAL

Altogether, he lost $4. His profit on the first horse was $18, but he lost $22 on the second horse.

313
THREE MAKES 18

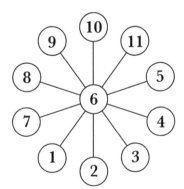

314
SIXTY MILES PER HOUR

There's no way to do it. Averaging 60 miles per hour, or a mile a minute, would mean that the 20-mile trip would take 20 minutes. However, the motorist has already used up 20 minutes on the first ten-mile leg of the trip: $1/2$ mile per minute x 10 miles = 20 minutes.

315
STRIPS OF PAPER

The cutting can be completed in 57 seconds. By putting the sheets together, so that all three are cut at the same time, it will take 19 cuts.

316
HOW MANY TRAINS?

25 trains. Just as she leaves Westville, she'll see a train pulling in that left Eastville at 9:00 P.M. the night before. When she reaches Eastville at 9:00 P.M. the next evening, she'll see a train just pulling out. During the trip, she will see 23 Westville-bound trains, from the one that left at 10:00 P.M. the night before to the one that departed at 8:00 P.M that same evening.

317
HOW OLD IS ANN?

Ann's mother is 25 years old, and Ann is four years and two months old.

318
FORTY POUNDS

The bar must be cut into four pieces that weigh one, three, nine, and 27 pounds. We'll list the methods for weighing one-through ten-pound objects and trust that you can take it from there:

	left pan:	right pan:
1	object	1 lb. piece
2	object + 1 lb.	3 lb.
3	object	3 lb.
4	object	3 lb. + 1 lb.
5	object + 1 lb. + 3 lb.	9 lb.
6	object + 3 lb.	9 lb.
7	object + 3 lb.	9 lb. + 1 lb.
8	object + 1 lb.	9 lb.
9	object	9 lb.
10	object	9 lb. + 1 lb.

319
GIVE AND TAKE

Jim had $50 and Jack had $30.

320
HOT AND COLD WATER

The tub will fill in five minutes. The cold faucet fills the tub in 400 seconds, and therefore fills $1/400$ of the tub in one second. Likewise, the hot faucet fills $1/480$ of the tub in one second. The tub empties $1/800$ of its contents in one second. Therefore:

$$1/400 + 1/480 - 1/800 = 1/300$$

That means $1/300$ of the tub is filled every second. Hence it would take 300 seconds, or five minutes, to fill the tub.

321
NICE IF YOU CAN GET IT

On the 28th day alone the worker would make $1,342,177.28.

322
A BIG DEAL IN FARM LAND

The farmer won. He sold a piece of land that was a straight line. Try drawing it if you'd like, using inches instead of miles.

323
DOLLARS AND CENTS

He started with $99.98 and spent $49.99.

324
AIRPLANE RACE

Plane B wins.
If, for example, the distance to the turning point is 84 miles, plane A would take 28 minutes going out and 21 minutes returning, or 49 minutes. Plane B would take only 48 minutes for the roundtrip.

325
THE ENTHUSIASTIC BEE

The bee traveled 20 miles. The riders would meet after each traveling half the 20-mile distance, or ten miles. At a rate of five miles per hour, that would take two hours. Since the bee was constantly traveling at ten miles per hour, he would log 20 miles in those two hours.

326
THE GUALALA WATER BOTTLE

The water costs $2^1/2$ cents, and the bottle 1.02^1/2$

327
HOW OLD WAS I?

I was 47. The only years that are practical with perfect square roots are 1849 and 1936. All others have roots that contain decimals. Taking 1849 from 1936 gives 87, which was my grandfather's age in 1936. In 1943 he would have been 94, so I would have been 47.

328
HOW LONG IS THE FOLD?

The fold AB is just a bit over $12^1/2$ inches long (12.529964).

329
THE HUNGRY CATS

Three minutes. Each cat finishes off one bowl in three minutes.

330
WEIGH THIS FISH

The fish weighs 20 pounds.

331
THE TWELVE-POINTED STAR

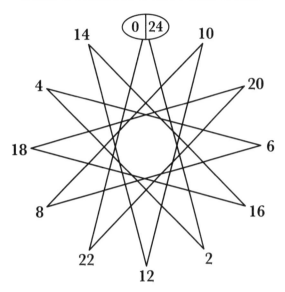

332
HARE AND HOUND

The hound makes up two feet every second, and his chase will take one minute to complete, so he was 120 feet away at the start. He completed only 50 seconds of his chase, so he'd made up only 100 feet when the hare went in his hole.

333
THE PEANUT-EATING MONKEYS

Five monkeys. If four monkeys can eat four sacks in three minutes, one monkey can eat one sack in three minutes. In 60 minutes, one monkey can eat 20 sacks. Thus it would take five monkeys to eat 100 sacks in 60 minutes.

334
HOW MANY STEPS?

11 steps:
steps 1–3: one foot
steps 4–6: two feet
steps 7–9: three feet
steps 10–11: five feet

335
THE THIRTY CENTS PUZZLE

There are five combinations:
1. six nickels
2. three dimes
3. one quarter and one nickel
4. four nickels and one dime
5. two nickels and two dimes

336
WHAT DID THE SUIT COST?

The suit cost $40.00.

337
JANE AND JOHN

Jane is 18 years old, and John is four.
When Jane becomes seven times as old
as John is now, or 28 years old, ten years
will have elapsed. John will then be 14,
so Jane will be twice his age.

338
GROWING PAINS

The father is 25 years old at present.

339
FILL UP THE TANK

45 minutes. It fills up $2/3$ as fast. Multiply
the inverse of that $3/2$ by 30 minutes.

340
LAWN MOWING

It will take him 30 minutes. Many people
will say one hour, assuming that the 50-
foot square is half the size. It's $1/4$ the
size, however.

341
HOW MANY MEN?

Three men were working. The job took
three days, or nine man-days. Therefore,
nine men could do it in one day.

342
THE BANK TELLER'S MISTAKE

The check was for $12.25. The teller
paid out $25.12. After 62 cents was
spent, there was $24.50 left.

343
THE FRIENDLY PROFESSOR

There were 21 handshakes, 15 between
the students and six from the professor.

344
SHE WAS THE MARRYING KIND

Nine. Each ex-husband attended with
the same ex-wife, the party's hostess.

345
HOW OLD IS ANN?...AGAIN

Ann is 24.

346
THE BILL

Mr. Rice began with eight one-dollar bills and Mr. Stutts had eight quarters. After the transfer of the $6, Mr. Stutts had $8 and Mr. Rice had $2.

347
PLAIN LIVING

44,616 different combinations

348
THE COUNTERFEIT PENNY

Five times:
1. Put 16 pennies in each pan of the scale. The lighter group is then divided into two groups of eight.
2. The eights are put in the pans and the lighter eight is then divided into fours.
3. Find the lighter four and divide it.
4. Find the lighter two and divide them.
5. Find the lighter one.

Although five weighings are needed to be sure, if you started with step 2, there's a 50% chance that the fake coin would be involved. If it was, you could then go to step 4, which gives you a 50% chance of being able to proceed to the final step. Doing it that way, you'd have a 50% chance of finding the fake in four steps and a 25% chance of finding it in three.

349
FASHION PARADE

There were 35 different combinations.

350
A PROBLEM IN SUBTRACTION

The digit is 2: 221 - 202 = 19

351
RAILROAD PROBLEM

210 (105 in each direction)

352
THE HUNDRED YEARS PUZZLE

Mrs. Green is 77, Mrs. Brown 44.

353
THE DRAWBRIDGE

They will meet 30 feet above the fully lowered position.

354
THE "TWICE AS MUCH" WILL

Betty: $3,000   Bob: $6,000
Brian: $12,000   Bill: $24,000

355
THE TWO AUTOMOBILES

The slower car needs a three-hour head start. Figure it by determining how long it would take each car to make the trip. The slower one would take 15 hours and the faster one 12 hours.

356
SOUR APPLES

He took 40 apples. The farmer got 20, his two sons got ten and five, in that order. That totals 35 apples. One more each for the three of them left two for the boy.

357
THE HIKERS

The slower one walked at 4 miles per hour, the faster one at $4^1/4$ miles per hour.

358
HE DID PRETTY WELL

His income was $60,000 a year.

359
TIRED AND RETIRED

He had 204 autos and 92 motorcycles.

360
CAPITAL GAINS

He will have $50,625.

361
COUNTING SHEEP

They both bought 40. That made the totals 210 to 70, or 3 to 1.

362
STEAMBOAT TRIP

120 miles each way

363
BROTHERS AND SISTERS

There were four boys and three girls.

364
1, 2, 3, 4, 5, 6, 7, 8, 9

2,520

365
A LITTER OF PIGS

The farmer had nine pigs.
$9 + 9 + 4^1/2 + 13^1/2 = 36$

366
THE CURIOUS CLOCK

65 minutes. Let's say the minute hand stops for a minute on the "12." Starting from the moment it resumes moving, it would take 60 minutes to circle the clock, plus a minute at each of these five times: 10 past, 20 past, 30 past, 40 past, and 50 past.

367
HOW MANY DUCKS?

There were three, one in front of another.

368
THREESCORE AND... ?

Her grandfather was 72 years old.

Cut-Outs

370
THE OCTAGON

Group each trio of pieces as shown, then put those four groups together to create the full shape.

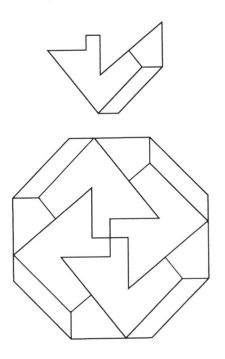

373
THE COMPLICATED SQUARE

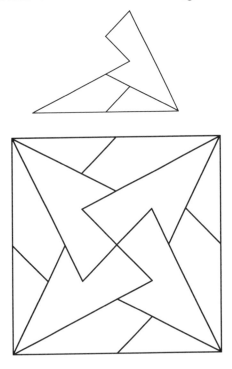

375
THE FIVE-PIECE CROSS

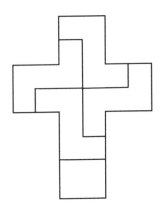

376
THE HOUSE AND PORCH

The two straight cuts are indicated by the solid lines. The dotted line, which bisects the bottom edge, is added to show the point where the two cuts meet.

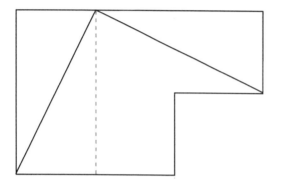

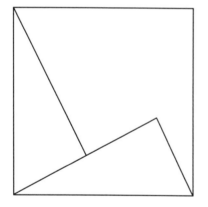

379
PLUS TO SQUARE

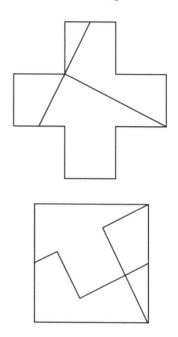

380
SQUARE TO OBLONG

Measure five $1/2$" increments going across the top and four $5/8$" increments going down. Then cut and move the pieces as shown.

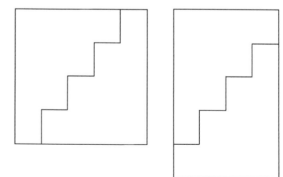

382
FIVE MAKE A CROSS

383
THE DIAMOND AND SQUARE

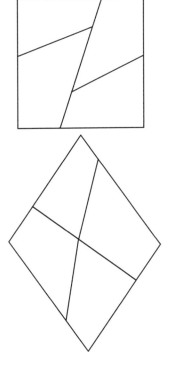

385
TORMENTORS

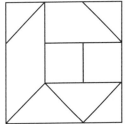

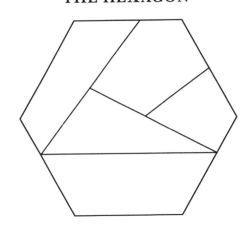

386
THE HEXAGON

387
CROSS-CUT

388
THE FOUR-PIECE SQUARE

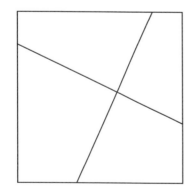

389
TRIANGLES AND SQUARE

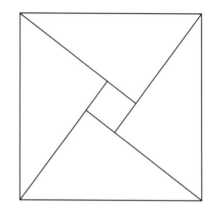

390
CUT-OUT STAR

Bonus

392
CHECKERBOARD PUZZLE

Here's one solution:

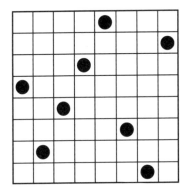

393
THE HANDCUFFS PUZZLE

Take the middle of one set of handcuffs and, narrowing it, thread it through the gap in one wrist loop. Now slip the threaded loop over the hand and then thread it out the other side of the wrist loop. The two sets of handcuffs will now be separated.

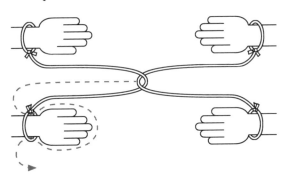

394
THE THREE DICE

Six, five, two, one

395
DICE SKYSCRAPERS

The total for the left skyscraper is 20, the total for the right is 18.

396
A PLAYING CARD PUZZLE

Here's one solution:

J-diam.	Q-club	K-heart	A-spade
K-spade	A-heart	J-club	Q-diam.
A-club	K-diam.	Q-spade	J-heart
Q-heart	J-spade	A-diam.	K-club

397
THE 10-CARD SQUARE

Here's one solution:

6	7	1	4
10			9
2	3	8	5

398
PLAYTIME PUZZLE CARDS

A. five-letter words:
1. maple
2. ample
3. empty
4. Italy
5. imply
6. pleat
7. metal
8. mealy
9. petal
10. meaty
11. plait
12. plate

B. names:
1. Ali, Amy, Eli, Lea, Mat, May, Mel, Mia, Pam, Pat, Pia, Tim (you may have found others)
2. Emily and Pat

C. four-letter words:
1. emit
2. item
3. lamp
4. malt
5. mail
6. mate
7. mile
8. palm
9. pate
10. peal
11. pelt
12. pity
13. plea
14. tale
15. tape
16. team
17. lame
18. type
19. Yale
20. yelp
21. pile
22. pale
23. melt
24. lime

D. timely, impale

400
THE FOUR HUNDREDTH

The remaining letters are E-N-D.

1. RED   2. F   3. HU   4. TH (twice)
5. OUR

Congratulations!

You've completed *Fabulous Fun With Puzzles*.